Somebody's
Child

Somebody's

The story of a man who found hope – and took it back to the streets

Child

John Robinson
with Jan Greenough

MONARCH
BOOKS

Oxford, UK & Grand Rapids, Michigan, USA

First published in the UK in 2007 by Monarch Books
(a publishing imprint of Lion Hudson plc),
Mayfield House, 256 Banbury Road, Oxford, OX2 7DH.
Tel: +44 (0) 1865 302750   Fax: +44 (0) 1865 302757
Email: monarch@lionhudson.com
www.lionhudson.com

ISBN: 978-1-85424-852-7 (UK)
ISBN: 978-0-8254-6149-1 (USA)

Distributed by:
UK: Marston Book Services Ltd, PO Box 269,
Abingdon, Oxon OX14 4YN;
USA: Kregel Publications, PO Box 2607,
Grand Rapids, Michigan 49501.

Unless otherwise stated, Scripture quotations are
taken from the Holy Bible, New International Version,
© 1973, 1978, 1984 by the International Bible Society.
Used by permission of Hodder and Stoughton Ltd.
All rights reserved.

The text paper used in this book has been made from wood inde-
pendently certified as having come from sustainable forests.

British Library Cataloguing Data
A catalogue record for this book is available
from the British Library.

Printed in and bound in Great Britain by Cox & Wyman Ltd, Reading.

CONTENTS

DEDICATION

To Gillian and my precious girls, Natalie and Leah:
I love you so much and pray that you will always
know you are not alone.

To everyone who feels alone in the world, as I did,
that you would know that you are somebody's child.

ACKNOWLEDGMENTS

Thank you to Gillian: not only am I grateful to have you in my life, but truly blessed to have such a good friend who has been with me through all the ups and downs. Thanks also to Gillian's family, for all your love and support.

I am also grateful to Jan Greenough: without your constant encouragement and phone calls we would not have been able to finish the book.

To those involved in the bus ministry who have given so much: without you we couldn't have reached so many young people for God.

Lastly, to everyone who has been working prayerfully and financially behind the scenes: you are a great support and strength. There are so many of you I couldn't begin to thank you all – you know who you are. God bless you.

John Robinson

FOREWORDS

The Eden Bus Ministry that John Robinson heads up works out of an office here at The Message Trust. A few days ago I was wandering through the office with another member of the team when I noticed a pile of books that John had been sent by his publisher. It was the latest batch of translations of John's life story, *Nobody's Child*, in Hungarian, Dutch, Korean and German. I said to my colleague, 'Isn't God amazing, that he can take someone like John, who was utterly broken, had no hope and was sleeping in shop doorways, and use them to bless the world?'

I'm sure that with the release of *Somebody's Child* even more people will be touched and inspired by John's ongoing journey. But I also know that what John longs for most of all is that through this important book, the most marginalized and hurting individuals will be given hope, and that their lives can also be turned round and set on a course that takes them, as Psalm 40 so poetically puts it, 'out of the slimy pit, out of the mud and mire, and sets their feet on a rock...so that many will see and fear and put their trust in the Lord'.

Every week here at The Message we gather all the

different teams working on the estates, in the schools and in the prisons across Greater Manchester for a time of prayer and encouragement. During these times John will invariably have a testimony to share with us about some tough young person who has encountered Jesus through the Bus Ministry. As he shares their difficult lives and the joy of salvation, we all love it and wait for John to say what has become his catchphrase – 'It brings a tear to your eye!' At this point a great cheer goes round the room.

Isn't it great that John's tears have gone from tears of brokenness and rejection to tears of joy over the salvation of needy young people just like him, and don't you just love the God who specializes in doing that with people, whether it be in South Korea, Holland, Thailand, Hungary, Germany or on the streets of Manchester?

Andy Hawthorne
Chief Executive, The Message Trust

John Robinson displays many gifts and talents whilst engaged in his varied ministries, including the Eden Bus, where he works with local young people in some of the most difficult areas of Greater Manchester. He has an amazing ability to share his personal experiences of hope and a changed life with the young people, who often feel hopeless and are sometimes on the edge of criminality. This is so refreshing in a world where others often spend hours agonizing over the best way to engage with young people – John just gets on and does it. *Somebody's Child* embodies this hope.

Alison Fletcher
Police Superintendent in Stockport
and previously in Salford

Chapter 1

LOOKING BACK

When *Nobody's Child* **was published,** I was amazed at the response. People bought that book and read it and lent it to their friends, and lots of them wrote to me and emailed me, telling me their own stories. You'll find some of them in this book, because God is still working in my life and in theirs, and what he does is always amazing. *Somebody's Child* tells the story of what has been happening since then. For those who haven't read *Nobody's Child*, this chapter fills in a bit of the background.

I never knew anything about my family when I was young. I grew up in care, and the social workers were careful not to give me much information. It was only when I was an adult, and discovered that the law allowed me to see my own records, that I was able to find out anything about my background. The records stated that neither of my parents wanted me: my father was in prison and my mother, an alcoholic, was living on benefits. When she went out drinking, she left the children locked in the house. By the time I was taken into care at five months old, I was already suffering from neglect.

Apparently I lived in several foster homes over the years, but every placement failed. I don't remember much about that: I only have vague memories of a couple of homes, and they aren't happy ones. In one of them I was beaten with a broom-handle, and in another I was forced to strip and smacked with a slipper. In one I slept in a bare attic divided into four cubicles, unable to play with the other three children locked in with me; when I wet the bed they made me eat mustard sandwiches, which made me sick. One day, after breakfast, my foster mother stripped me naked and put me in the cellar, and left me there all day in the dark and cold while she went to work.

Eventually, when I was about nine years old, I was sent to a Barnardo's home in Tadcaster, a few miles outside York. That home was the closest I ever got to family life, and the staff tried hard to give us the kind of love, security and guidance that children need. I was happy there. My only real sadness was that no one in my family had ever tried to make contact with me. Other kids received presents and cards on their birthdays; I only ever had a card from the staff. Every year, at Christmas and birthdays, that rejection by my family was rubbed in, until it seemed to shape my whole life. Even among the other children in care, I stood out as the boy nobody wanted.

As I grew up I realized that being a Barnardo's boy was always going to mark me out. At secondary school there was a stigma attached to being in care, and girls didn't want to go out with me. Later on I got lazy about studying and my school-work began to suffer. There didn't seem to be any point in trying to prepare for the future when no one took any interest in me. I wanted so much to belong to a group and have friends of my own, and I started hanging around with some older lads in the town.

We used to climb over a fence at the back of the Yorkshire breweries and collect reject beer cans with dents in them, and we had a great time drinking and being rowdy. As we got older we got cocky, off-loading a crate here and there. We were cautioned a few times by the police, but no one took it too seriously. Then one night we lifted some beer and went out to a nearby barn to drink it. While we were messing around a candle fell over into a bale of straw, and to our horror the whole barn went up in flames. The police arrived, and I was charged with arson. Even though I told everyone it was an accident, I was found guilty and sentenced to six weeks in a detention centre.

The detention centre was horrible: I was only fourteen, and most of the time I was terrified. I got beaten up a lot and started wetting the bed again, which made the bullying worse. When I was released I was glad to get back home to Barnardo's, and I vowed that I was never going to get into trouble again. Then the blow fell: as soon as I turned sixteen I would have to leave – my place was needed for a younger child.

Leaving Barnardo's seemed like the end of the world. I left school at the same time – what was the point of taking exams when I already had a criminal record? No one would ever give me a job. Emotionally I was still very immature, and I had no idea how to take care of myself. Once again I started hanging out with the wrong lads, drinking in the pub and trying to look big. They were all involved in crime – shoplifting and stealing cars – and I went along with it. It felt like adventure, and I thought it was exciting. We did a couple of burglaries of commercial premises – we never did houses, but we reckoned the shops could afford to lose a bit, and anyway the insurance companies would pay.

I lived in a squat with a group of my mates, and it was horrible – filthy and smelling of vomit and urine. Most of the people there were on drugs, and you could get hold of anything if you wanted it. I tried LSD once but it gave me terrible nightmares, so I kept off it. In spite of acting big, I was often afraid – fights could break out over nothing. I felt I needed to be in control if I was going to take care of myself.

I was always wary and on edge, because you never knew what would happen next. Sometimes it was a raid by another gang, looking for a fight. Sometimes it was a raid by the police, looking for drugs or stolen goods. We always seemed to be running away from something. I carried a Bowie knife – a dagger with a blade about a foot long – and I set about establishing a reputation for toughness, getting tattoos and acting big. Only I knew that inside I wasn't tough at all. I was living a hard, fast, dangerous life, and sometimes I was sure I would die from it: one fight too many, picked with the wrong person, and that would be it. I was mixing with a criminal crowd, and they were all in and out of prison all the time. They were violent, too. I lost count of the number of times I was admitted to hospital with stab wounds, bruises or cuts that needed stitches. I've got some dramatic scars. Every time I tried to leave the gang I was beaten up. It was a terrible life but I didn't know how to get out, and I didn't know anyone outside it. I was on my own – what choice did I have?

I ended up in prison for burglary – and that was so awful that I tried to commit suicide. When I came out after eighteen months I slipped back into my old ways, mainly because there was no support to help me find a job or anywhere to live, and after a while I was arrested yet again. I could see that I was sliding down the slope towards becoming one of the old lags I'd met in jail – men who had drifted in and out of prison all their lives.

Then I got a lucky break from a compassionate judge who offered me one more chance: a Conditional Discharge, which meant that I was released to a bail hostel. This time I wasn't going to blow it. I got a job, I kept the rules, and I started putting my life back together. It nearly worked, too. I got a good job in a factory. I met a girl and got married, and even bought a house. I had a wife and good friends, and I thought I really had it made. Then, just like before, everything fell apart.

One night when I was working the late shift I realized I'd left my sandwiches at home and went back for them. I found my wife at home with my best friend, at two o'clock in the morning. I felt sure that they were having an affair. I couldn't cope with the shock, so I just walked out and left everything, even my job. I felt the betrayal more keenly, I think, because I had always felt so alone. I'd dreamt all my life of having a family of my own, and now it had all been snatched away again. I went back on the streets, living rough and getting into fights, nearly starving and not caring what happened to me. One doctor who stitched up my cuts was so concerned about my depressed state of mind that he sent me to a mental hospital for a while, but when I came out I was still living the same hopeless, lonely life as before. Nobody cared about me.

I slept on the street if I couldn't find a squat or a mate with a spare floor; sometimes I managed to get a place in a hostel. Some of those hostels were truly awful places, with big gates and barbed wire round the walls – more to keep the local vandals out than to keep the residents in. Often they were used as 'resettlement centres' for recovering drug addicts and alcoholics, as well as hostels for the homeless, and lots of the men were in a bad way. Some drank meths when they couldn't get hold of anything else, and several were incontinent and always vomiting. No matter how much disinfectant was used, the place always smelt bad. I could see why so many of the residents found it hard to give up the habits that were destroying them – it was their only way of escape from the awful reality of their lives.

We were all unemployed. One of our problems was that the hostels had a really bad reputation, so even when there were jobs available, no one would take us on when they knew where we were living. For a while I went round with a sack, collecting old cans and using a magnet to find out if they were aluminium – you could make a bit of money that way. Spending the day walking round searching the ground for other people's rubbish made me think, 'I'm just a piece of rubbish myself.' I felt so alone.

I met all sorts of people in those hostels – some of

them were 'men of the road', who walked from town to town, staying in hostels in the winter months and sleeping outside when it was warmer. Many of them weren't so bad, and they still had some self-esteem and a kind of dignity. Others were deeply depressed and in despair, men who would drink or smoke or inject almost anything to achieve oblivion. One man didn't do drugs or alcohol but he was always cutting himself: his emotional state was so bad that self-harming was the only way he could express his pain.

I never wanted to do that, but I could understand him. When no one cares about you, you don't care about yourself. There had been times in my life when I didn't care whether I lived or died. I thought I'd escaped from that sort of despair once, and yet here I was again at the bottom of the pile. What hope was there now that anyone would ever take an interest in me?

It was while I was living like this, drifting from hostel to hostel, that God reached out and put his hand on me. I'd been taken to church as a child, but I thought religion was pretty boring, really, so when I came across some Christians singing in the street I wasn't interested. But one of them came over and started talking to me, and invited me to a meeting in the Town Hall. I don't know why I went – except that they all looked so happy, and the man, Tony, seemed genuinely interested in me. 'Jesus loves you,' he said, and somehow it didn't sound stupid when he said it. All I'd ever wanted was someone to love me and make me feel I was a real person, and now his words re-awakened this terrible longing in me.

I went to the meeting and I met God – that's the only way I can explain it. I suddenly understood, without a doubt, that although nobody on this earth seemed to care about me, God did. Even though I had been a criminal and a fighter and I'd never lived the way God wanted me to, he didn't blame me. Jesus had taken all the blame for me, and I could make a fresh start if I really wanted to. All I had to do was accept his love.

There were tears pouring down my face. I felt as if God was saying, 'John, you're special to me.' It was a fantastic feeling. I thought, 'I've been stabbed and beaten and people have robbed things off me, but no one can take God away from me.'

That was the moment when I became a Christian. I put my life in God's hands, without any idea where it might lead me. At that time, just knowing God's love was enough. I didn't have any expectations about how it was going to change my life.

In fact, God was leading me out of the hopeless pit my life had become, to a place where I could be useful for him, but it wasn't an easy journey. I'd never lived in a real home, and I didn't know how to trust people. I needed to gain some self-esteem, to learn how to be responsible and considerate, and how to take part in the give and take of family life. God lined up some wonderful Christians to play a part in helping me. Tony and his wife Sylvia in Sittingbourne, the Network Team in Deptford, Joey and Bridie the travellers, Julie and Ian on the Isle of Wight, and the community at Lee Abbey all took me in, one after another, and led me along the road to a life where I mattered.

I grew as a Christian, studying the Bible and taking courses in discipleship with the Ichthus Christian Fellowship. I got involved in soup runs, serving the homeless in the East End of London – it wasn't so long since I'd been scavenging in bins myself. For the first time in years there was a purpose to my life. I learned about forgiveness, and went through the pain and emotional healing of learning to forgive all the people who had hurt me.

I stayed with Tony and Sylvia for about a year, and living in their home taught me a lot. I'll never forget them because their love and care gradually chipped away some of my rough edges and taught me how to live with other people as a family. It couldn't have been easy for them, because when they took me in I was in a terrible state – physically unwell and emotionally exhausted. I tested them out a bit, because I couldn't believe that they could really love me. One night I went out and got really drunk and was sick on the floor. All they said was, 'We still love you, John, but you've got to clean up the mess yourself.' They showed me that I had to take responsibility for my actions, and helped me to grow as a person. They really lived out the love of God, and they helped me to understand God's unconditional love for us.

It sounds so easy to say that God changed my life, but it wasn't quick and it wasn't simple. Just as my body was marked by the life I'd led – covered in tattoos as well as scars from the beatings and stabbings – so my mind and my emotions were scarred by the loneliness, the rejections, the years of hoping and longing for love. I was used to pushing people away and putting up barriers because I couldn't face getting hurt all over again. Sometimes I found it difficult when we talked in the study group about drugs, alcohol, divorce, and all the other things that damage people's lives, because I was still sensitive about lots of things. Sometimes my tears were very near the surface as I spoke about the effect those things had had on my own life, but I felt safe and protected with my new friends around me and praying with me. Those Christians in the Fellowship became the brothers and sisters I'd never had, and I found a burning passion to share the love of Jesus with other people. I knew it could transform lives.

Lee Abbey in particular was a great place to grow as a Christian, because when you live in a community you can't hide your feelings or pretend anything. I learned self-discipline (for example, getting up on time and preparing properly when it was my turn to lead a prayer meeting), tolerance and love. That was when God gave me an even greater gift, the one thing I had always longed for – someone who was special to me and who loved me for myself.

I met Gillian when she was staying at Lee Abbey for a couple of months as a 'working guest' – someone who lives and works alongside the community but isn't a permanent part of it. We used to go for long walks on the hills and beach, and as we got to know each other, I began to realize that this was more than just a friendship. I was afraid to ask her out – I told her that I couldn't do that unless she promised it would be serious. I was terrified of being hurt and let down yet again if I let myself love someone, but deep down we both knew that the feelings we had for each other were very special.

Something we had in common was a deep sense of vocation. Gillian had known from the age of fourteen that God wanted her to be ordained as a minister, but at that time her paster didn't agree with women's ministry. By the time she went back home to Southampton we knew we wanted to get married.

At last I knew it was time to move on again, to take up my responsibilities in the real world. I'd learned a lot, but most of all I knew with absolute certainty that Jesus would walk with me every day and be my constant companion. That gave me the courage to start the next phase of my life. I moved to Southampton and took a job as a care worker in a special school, and helped with the youth programme in the church where Gillian worked. We had a wonderful wedding and settled down to married life, doing our best to serve God in the work he had given us.

It was while we were in Southampton that I first got the idea for a bus ministry. I'd done some research for the local churches into why young people didn't go to church, and I knew they thought the church was irrelevant to them. I wanted to take the gospel out to the streets where they were hanging out with their mates, and I hit on the idea of getting a camper van which I could drive round the estates, offering them a place to sit and talk and have a hot drink. We got funding from the Bishop of Winchester, I collected a group of helpers, and soon the Streetwise project was up and running.

The van was popular with the kids. As they began

to trust us, they started to ask why we put so much effort into helping them, and we were able to tell them about Jesus. A number of them became Christians.

Meanwhile, Gillian still felt a strong calling to be ordained, and after a great deal of prayer she applied and was accepted at theological college in Bristol. We passed on the care of the Streetwise work to a colleague, and moved house. I took a job as a youth and children's worker while Gillian went to college. Leah, our first child, was born halfway through the course, and Gillian used to study with her books on top of the table and one foot rocking the baby underneath! I was studying, too, for a higher diploma in Youth and Community Work. I knew that I had to be properly qualified if I was going to continue doing this work that meant so much to me. It was a struggle. Several times I threw an essay into the fire in disgust because my dyslexia made writing so hard for me. I was over the moon when I got my diploma: ordinary John Robinson, brought up in care and knocked about on the streets, had achieved something special!

We went back to Southampton, where the Bishop had plans for us: a church where we could work together, where Gillian could exercise her gifts for ministry and I could run the youth work. Gillian worked as a curate in the church and I got out on the streets again, meeting young people, doing school visits, and setting up a new Streetwise project, on the same lines as the first one.

Life wasn't all plain sailing. Gillian had had a grumbling appendix for some time, and eventually, when the pain got very bad, she was taken into hospital for investigations. She was on the emergency surgery list for twenty-four hours, but there wasn't a slot for her, and I took Leah home because we didn't want her to see her mummy in such distress. I was at home, looking after Leah, when the appendix burst and the emergency operation was finally performed. There were complications – one lung collapsed and she developed a blood infection – and she became very seriously ill. For a while we didn't know if she would live or die, and I was desperate. Was I going to lose her? I was filled with such fear that my precious family might be snatched away from me again. Still, I held on to the fact that God was in charge. Whatever happened, he wouldn't desert me. I kept praying, and gradually Gillian pulled through.

When our second daughter Natalie was born, we had to juggle two children and two part-time jobs between us. Life was certainly complicated and challenging, but we knew we were doing God's will, and neither of us was afraid of hard work. We were happy and busy and looking forward to the future, but we had no idea what God was planning for us next.

Chapter 2

CATCHING THE VISION

By **1999 my life was different** from anything I'd ever known. I had my own family, with two little girls who were mine, and so precious to me. I had a lovely wife who had her own calling and a strong relationship with God. I had my work with young people. And most of all, I had Jesus. This was something that had changed my life, but getting used to a different way of thinking was still a challenge. For as long as I could remember, I had lived with rejection as part of who I was. It was all I had ever known, and learning to live without it, and learning to trust God instead, was like taking the first steps on a journey – one I'm still making.

I had been a nobody all my life, nobody's child, and a person that nobody cared about. I knew now that I was somebody to God. That was clear in my mind from the moment I became a Christian – but I was still learning that I was a family man, cared for by my family, and I had to understand what that meant. For instance, if I was having a bad day I would go off on my own for the whole afternoon, just driving around or going for a long walk, and switch off my phone so no one could get in touch. It never occurred to me that Gillian might worry about me. I'd never had to consider anyone else's feelings like that. Nowadays I've learned that lesson, and I stay in touch.

One problem was that I was so terrified of being rejected that I used to get in first – I used to push people away before they rejected me. Gillian found that hard when we were first married, because she didn't understand what I was doing. Fortunately God understands what we need, and at that point he brought our friend Trish into Gillian's life to be a friend to her. Trish had lived with me in the community at Lee Abbey, so she knew me well. She understood the hurt I had been through and the ways I tended to deal with it, so she was able to pray with Gillian about it.

Getting upset like that was something that used to happen if we had even the smallest argument, because whenever I made a mistake I was always afraid that I'd blown it – I used to think that I was about to lose everything all over again. I had to learn that married couples have their disagreements, and that there are ways of talking about things and sorting them out, and making up after a row.

We had a lot of talking to do around that period, because Gillian's time as a curate was coming to an end. We always knew that we would be moving on from Southampton eventually, because ministers in the Anglican Church only serve as a curate for a maximum of four years. Gillian had spent three years in her first church; then in the fourth year she was moved to another parish within the team ministry, where she was curate-in-charge. That meant it was rather like being the vicar for that church, but with the team rector overseeing the whole team. It was a good dry run for her first post as a vicar, as she was free to work alone, but with the support of the team ministry behind her.

She enjoyed working there. It was a small, beautiful church with a friendly congregation, and plenty of opportunities to work with young families in particular. Preparing and leading three services on a Sunday as well as all the rest of the tasks involved in church ministry meant that it was hard work but very rewarding, and the church was growing. Towards the end of that year, as we were both praying about where God would lead us next, a friend in the church took Gillian aside.

'Whose job will you follow when you move on,' she said, 'yours or John's? You won't be able to get a job together.'

'Both,' said Gillian. She had it set in her mind that God would show us where to go, and that he would give us both work in the same place, however unlikely it sounded. The world was open to us and we would go wherever he wanted us. We tried not to be too anxious, just to trust God and keep praying. One day Gillian was praying while she did the ironing and she said to God, 'Lord, I'm tired of all this uncertainty. I really want to know, now, where we'll be going.' A few minutes later the phone rang. It was David Gillett, who had been the Principal of her theological college and was now the Bishop of Bolton. He said to her, 'How do you fancy coming up to work in this diocese?'

'I don't mind,' said Gillian. 'I'll go wherever God wants.'

'Well, a couple of parishes here have vacancies. What about coming and having a look?'

She travelled up alone to look around, while I stayed and looked after the children. She came home full of enthusiasm.

I had been looking around for my next step too. The week before, I had taken a group of our young people from Southampton to camp at Soul Survivor at Shepton Mallet. It's a Christian festival which offers worship, teaching and music in a style that young people can relate to. The kids loved it because it spoke to them in their own language, and they were amazed to see so many Christians in one place, camping in the grounds, listening to the music, studying the Bible and praising God together. They liked the bands, too, especially The World Wide Message Tribe. They thought it was really cool to see hundreds of young people jumping up and down to 'Jumping in the House of God'.

I was just as excited as they were. I could see that The Tribe were getting over their message about God in a way that our kids could understand. Then a guy got up and started talking about how we could live our lives for God, and I thought he was really good, too. It was Andy Hawthorne, who headed the band and led The Message Trust.

After their set I went back and found Andy. I explained who I was, and about my Bus Ministry in Southampton. 'It's all about getting out and meeting young people on the street, and talking in language they understand,' I said. 'Just like The Tribe. Would you be willing to come and play for us in Southampton?'

'OK,' said Andy, 'if you'll do something in return. I think you might be the man we need to come and head up our Bus Ministry in Manchester. Will you think about it?'

I was pretty surprised, but I said I would. His talk had been inspiring. His theme was 'no more hit and run' – the sort of evangelism where people visit an area to preach the gospel, but then leave and go back to their own (more comfortable) surroundings. He talked about not just preaching the message but also living it: actually moving house to the places where God's word is needed and living out your faith. The teams of people on the Eden Project did just that, living and working in some of the toughest areas of Manchester, not just for a year, but for life. It was a vocation.

I hadn't heard about this kind of evangelism for a long time, and it struck a chord with me. I'd been taking my bus onto the streets of Southampton to catch up with young people in the places where they were hanging out with their friends, the sort of kids who wouldn't go to a church youth club if you paid them. Now here was Andy talking about living life alongside the kids on the estates of Manchester. I caught his vision, and it made perfect sense to me. The Bus Ministry was planned to support the Eden teams; the bus would provide a sort of mobile youth centre which could visit areas where there was nowhere for kids to meet up.

I wondered if this was the next step for me. Andy said he felt that God was telling him I was the man they wanted – but it was no good unless I felt it as well. I asked for time to talk to Gillian, to think and pray with her about it.

One of the first things I did was to go up and visit The Message in Manchester – I knew I had to see it to understand the nature of the work. I stayed in one of the Eden Project houses, on one of the deprived estates, and I had a good look round and talked to some of the volunteers. At the time I was working with churches in the New Forest, where there were some very well-off areas with posh houses and tree-lined streets – a far cry from the scruffy social housing and concrete walkways of the Manchester estates. I came to the conclusion that the only difference was that in Manchester, what you see is what you get. The area looked poor and deprived, and it was. In the New Forest in the affluent south, there might be a bit more money about, but this often disguised the real problems. People might not be out of work or short of money, but so many of them were still short of love. Kids still went off the rails and experimented with drink and drugs. Housing was more expensive, so young people stood no chance of being able to afford a home of their own. Often they were disillusioned and displaced, with no sense of community.

In any case, wherever you get people, you get similar problems. Family break-ups, drink and drug problems, loneliness, unemployment, a sense that no one cares – these are the same wherever you live. The difference in Manchester was that there was more poverty and a higher crime rate – whatever the causes, the two tend to map together pretty closely. It made life on the estates all the more challenging.

I found out a bit about The Message, too. It started in 1988, when Andy and his brother ran their first youth mission. They had a vision to reach the young people in Manchester for God, and using the biggest rock venue in the city seemed to be a successful way of doing it. Then Mark Pennells, a friend of Andy's, came along. He had been in a band, but had become disillusioned with record deals and big gigs, and he wanted to use his musical gift to share Jesus. Together they set up 'The Message to Schools', doing school assemblies and lunchtime concerts and preaching in the evening – Mark doing the music and Andy preaching. The band evolved, with Andy adding some rapping. They got some people in to sing and some dancers as well, and in 1991 'The World Wide Message Tribe' was born.

The Tribe got more and more successful, but their priority was always the schools in Manchester. Even when they had big recording contracts and were known all over the Christian world, they went on performing in the toughest schools. Once they turned down the chance to perform to 70 million people on international TV, because they were booked to play at a school in Ramsbottom!

One year they ran a mission in Wythenshawe, in south Manchester, and at the end of two weeks they gave a fantastic concert where around 100 kids responded to the gospel. The mission team did what they always did – referred them to the local church – and all 100 turned up on the Sunday! Unfortunately, it was a tiny church of about twenty people – faithful Christians, but quite unable to cope with discipling those numbers. Especially when they were ordinary kids with no church background, whose habits and approach were poles apart from the church. A few of the young people stuck with it, but most of them drifted away.

Andy and the others could see what the problem was: the toughest areas of the city, where the problems and the needs were greatest, were also the areas with the fewest Christians. Any mission they ran in these challenging areas of deprivation, hardship and crime would face the same problem: not enough churches to carry on the long-term work once the mission was over. What was needed was a task force, but not one that went in and out again. They needed groups of Christians who would live and work in those districts. It took a lot of planning and preparation, but the first Eden Project was set up in Wythenshawe in 1997.

Others followed, and they have all been different in minor ways, but they all have four basic elements in common: they're rooted in a local church; they're focused on the toughest neighbourhoods; they include a large team of Christians who are willing to establish their homes in the heart of the community; and they make young people their top priority.

The teams are not professional evangelists: they are ordinary people, living out their ordinary lives in their new communities. They aren't paid: they have to find jobs and housing, just like their neighbours. The difference is that they are Christians, so they find ways to help their community through social action and preaching and living the gospel.

What happened in a short space of time was that

crime rates in Wythenshawe fell, the atmosphere of the neighbourhood improved and even house prices began to rise. The local police spotted the trend straight away and realized that some of the most active young troublemakers on their patch had found something that was drawing them away from crime. The church was making a difference.

Since then eight other Eden Projects have been started, all in deprived and volatile areas where drug and alcohol abuse, gangs, fighting, crime and other social problems abound. The idea of a mobile youth centre where young people could meet their friends, listen to music, watch DVDs and talk to Christian volunteers, seemed like a brilliant way of supporting the work. I came home from Manchester really excited.

It was certainly looking like a job I would love to do, but I couldn't make that decision alone. I had my family to consider, and Gillian and I make all our plans together. We sat down to pray about it.

One of the great things about our marriage is also one of the most difficult things – we have both had our own ministries from the start. Gillian has her ministry as a vicar, while mine is for outreach, in my role as a youth worker, but we both have the same heart for taking the gospel of Jesus to the people who need him, whether in the church or on the street. Occasionally (as in the non-alcoholic bar we established at our church in Southampton) our activities overlap, and we find ourselves working side by side. The rest of the time our ministries and activities are different, though our aims are the same. In our busy schedules, we struggle to make time to be together.

Before we had children, sustaining two ministries was fine. Afterwards it became more of a challenge. Gillian's Director of Training in Southampton once suggested to her that as a mum of two children, maybe she should stay at home and just support me in my work. She replied, 'That sounds lovely, but it isn't what God has asked me to do. Most of the time I would really love to be at home all day – but I know God has put me here to do this job, and I'll go on doing it as best I can.'

It has always meant that we live in a fairly high-pressure world, but we know this is where God wants us to be. Often in Southampton I felt it would be nice if we could spend Friday or Saturday evenings together, like most couples – but in youth work those are the most important nights. We never had much in the way of evenings together, even at weekends. But as Gillian said, philosophically, 'It's one of those things you do for God, really.' We were both busy and committed to giving our lives to God, and we did the best we could to support each other and make sure that the girls got a fair share of our time.

Right now, everything seemed to be coming together. I went through The Message's thorough interviewing system, and a couple of days later Andy Hawthorne rang me to confirm the offer of the job. Gillian and I could see that Manchester would be a good place for both of us, and God had done what he had promised – he had sorted us out two jobs in the same place. I was going to be the Eden Bus Manager, and Gillian was going to be the part-time priest-in-charge of a church in a small town on the edge of

Manchester. We would be living in a vicarage that was close enough to The Message for me to travel to work.

We had mixed feelings about leaving Southampton. Of course we were excited about what God had in store for us, but at the same time we would be sad to leave so many good friends, and the work we had been building up for the last few years. I was happy to be going back up north – even if it was the wrong side of the Pennines! – but Gillian had always lived in the south of England, apart from her time at Edinburgh University. I wondered how different she would find it.

It had never mattered much to me where I lived, because I never had any family base, so I had no one to visit. Most of Gillian's family lived in Cambridgeshire, so the journey from Manchester to visit them wouldn't be much different from the journey from Southampton. Gillian's real sadness was leaving her grandma and grandad, who lived relatively close to us in Portsmouth, so we had been able to visit them quite regularly. They would miss seeing us and their great-granddaughters. I was sad to leave them, too. When I first met them, they really weren't sure what to make of me, but they got to know me and we got on really well. Grandma once said to me, 'You're like a grandson to me,' and that acceptance meant a lot. She was so proud when my first book was published that she told everyone about it! I'm so glad she and grandad were able to read it and be proud of me before they died.

Still, everything else was falling into place. We packed ourselves up and set off for the north. The next phase in our family life was beginning.

Chapter 3

SETTLING IN

Our move was just as mad as our lives always seemed to be. We set off with all our belongings packed in the removal vans, and two very excited little girls in the back of the car. Leah and Natalie were four and two, and they didn't fully understand what a big change was happening in all our lives – all they knew was that it was a very long journey.

We got as far as Winchester when the exhaust started making a very strange noise, and we realized that we needed urgent repairs. We drove the car to a garage and begged them to fix it – and they agreed, since it was clear that we were en route somewhere, with the car filled to bursting with boxes and bags. We gathered the girls and stood watching from a safe distance as the mechanic raised the car onto a ramp over the inspection well. Then we heard the most terrible yowling, so loud that the mechanic stopped the lifting mechanism, because he thought an animal had somehow been run over. It was our cat Louis, still in his cat box on the back seat, and protesting at the strange sensation of going up in a lift! We rescued him, got the car mended and went on our way northwards, much delayed.

Our first impressions were that we were moving to a beautiful area. Our new home was just on the edge of Manchester, and we passed through some wonderful countryside, with high, wild-looking hills and moorland, before we reached the town set in a valley. It was an old mill town, and though some of the warehouses had been converted into smart modern flats, the town itself was still a very ordinary, mostly working-class area. It had chip-shops and pubs and a railway line, with steep streets of grey stone cottages and small brick houses.

The other thing we noticed very quickly was the climate. People had told me it always rained in Manchester, and I didn't believe them – but they were right! It seemed to rain almost every day that autumn. The weather came straight in off the Atlantic, and the clouds dropped all their rain on us before setting off across the Pennines to the rest of the country.

Unfortunately, it turned out that the house we had been allocated by the diocese wasn't in Gillian's new parish at all. For complicated reasons to do with the movement of clergy, another family was living in the vicarage in our parish. We had to be housed temporarily in a different vicarage four miles away, which wasn't an ideal arrangement for a new vicar trying to get to know the church family. Gillian had to travel to the church for services and meetings, some of her new congregation felt abandoned because their vicar wasn't living locally, and it was specially difficult to become a part of 'our' community. Meanwhile, some of the local people resented us being in 'their' vicarage, as we weren't serving their parish. It was to be three years before we moved on, but it was hard to put down roots because we always thought we would move soon. Still, it was a pleasant house and we did our best to settle in. It was a strange sort of 'limbo' time, waiting to move into our real new home, at the heart of the parish where Gillian needed to be.

This arrangement also meant that Leah couldn't start school in our new parish, because technically we were living outside the catchment area. We thought that perhaps this might be a good thing. Gillian would automatically be a governor of the church school, and would be going in to lead assemblies and so on, and Leah might find it embarrassing to have her mum around as the vicar of her school! Fortunately we found another school for her nearby, and it turned out to be a very popular and sought-after church school.

Eventually the good news arrived – the vicarage in our own parish was free. It was right next to the church, so we would be on the spot for all activities and services.

Meanwhile, we'd all been getting used to our new surroundings. I well remember when I first left Yorkshire and moved south: people used to take the mickey out of my accent and pretend not to understand me. Now Gillian was the one who was a novelty: she only had to open her mouth and people would say, 'She's not a northerner, is she?' (In fact, these days she has acclimatized quite well, and a few northern phrases have even crept into her sermons!) But I can walk into a shop and say, 'Hello, love,' and no one bats an eyelid. People also called her, jokingly, a 'southern softy' because she was always complaining about the cold. There were one or two strange things with the local language that made us laugh: Gillian was puzzled by people who said, 'Can I give you a lift?' when they knew she had her own car and could drive herself anywhere she wanted. It was a long while before someone explained that in the north, this meant 'Can I give you a hand? Do you want some help?'

Our new church was tiny, with a congregation of around twenty on an average week. They were prayerful people, which was wonderful, and they had managed to keep going in spite of their small numbers and the threat of merging and losing their own minister. They were used to very traditional services, and we could see that there would be some hard decisions ahead. Gillian had a vision for this tiny church. She could see that it wasn't meeting the needs of people in the area – there would have been more people coming to church if it was – yet those traditional services were the preferred form of worship for that faithful remnant of people who had kept the church going for years. We both have a strong urge for mission, and a belief that the church should be spreading the good news of Jesus to everyone. That means reaching out to the unchurched majority – and those are the very people to whom traditional church services mean very little.

We prayed together about our new church family and Gillian's responsibilities. Her vision was for a church where everyone was welcome, an honest place where everyone could grow and learn together. How could she go about meeting the needs of the people within the church, but at the same time reach out and meet the needs of those outside?

Back in Manchester I reported for duty at The Message, not at all sure what was going to be expected of me. For one thing, I didn't know how to drive a bus, so I had to learn. I didn't need a PSV (Passenger Service Vehicle) licence, since we weren't going to carry passengers, but I did need some intensive instruction in how to handle a large vehicle. The bus is forty feet long and eight feet wide, and it weighs around fourteen tonnes. It's not an easy thing to drive, and I spent a hair-raising weekend manoeuvring round the city streets, reversing, going round tight corners and learning to park in a city where I didn't know my way around. It's hard enough to drive a car or ride a bike round Manchester, let alone drive a monster like that. It was such a relief when my instructor told me that I'd passed the test, and I drove back to the office in high spirits.

At that time The Message was located in an old warehouse in Cheadle, which we shared with some other organizations. Our offices were upstairs, and mine was by the fire escape and some rather smelly toilets, so it wasn't exactly glamorous. Still, I had a photo taken with Andy and the team to send to the kids in Southampton. They had been very excited about my new job, thinking I was going to be famous, and saying, 'John's going to work with the Tribe!' I had to keep saying, 'No, I'm going to work for The Message – it's a lot bigger than just the Tribe,' but of course the band was the big thing in their eyes.

In fact The Message was getting bigger: the Eden

teams were in place and growing, and the schools work was increasing too, and it all needed staff to make the arrangements and handle the administration. As the work got bigger, our office space felt smaller: when all twenty-five of us met together for prayer, it was 'Open all the windows and sit on someone's lap!'

Another complication was that although we had a bus – a huge red double-decker – we didn't have anywhere to garage it on site. We had to park it in a haulage yard about fifteen miles away, and that meant a lot of travelling to and fro. I had to learn to be more organized: it was no good going out to work on the bus and then finding I'd left something important in the office.

The story of that first bus was a fascinating one. John and Rose Lancaster are a wonderful couple, vibrant Christians and long-term supporters of The Message. John is a businessman who is known for his faithful charitable giving. They had attended a fundraising dinner at the Manchester United Football Club, where they had heard Andy speaking about his vision for The Message and the projects planned for the next few years. One of them was the Bus Ministry. He described how it would work, and how a bus would enable The Message to get out on the streets and provide youth-club-style facilities to kids who wouldn't normally get the chance to enjoy them. He told them that the bus would support the Eden teams by drawing in the local youngsters, and would give the volunteers the opportunity to share the gospel and show them the love of Christ. Andy realized it might be a while before this dream could become a reality, of course, because it would cost a lot – in the region of £90,000. He hoped that the fund-raising dinner would take a step – however small – towards achieving that dream.

The idea rang bells for John and Rose. They knew how great the needs were in Manchester, and they loved the idea of bringing the youth work to the young people instead of expecting them to conform to the old-fashioned 'church youth club' pattern. They looked at each other, and John got to his feet.

'I've got a bit of a confession to make,' he began, in his blunt northern accent. 'We've been busy for the last couple of weeks – so busy that I forgot to buy my wife a birthday present! But Andy's given me an idea. I think I'll buy her a bus! Go ahead and get your bus, Andy. And we'll cover the cost.'

He was as good as his word: funds were transferred to The Message and the big double-decker bus was duly purchased. Rose was thrilled – especially when she came down to the yard to see 'her' bus, and found that we'd fixed to the bonnet a specially made number plate with the word 'ROSIE' on it! All we had to do now was fit it out.

The budget was better than anything I had ever dreamed of back in the days of my little camper van in Southampton. A whole team of us got together to work out what we wanted, what we needed, what was practical and what wasn't. For instance, we decided that we couldn't have a toilet on the bus (useful though that would have been for us), because it would have to be a chemical toilet, and we'd have to drive to a depot every night to empty it. And anyway, for the bus to be a safe environment, it was important that it was a single open space, with nowhere for anyone to hide or be out of sight. A toilet would be the one place where you couldn't see what the young people might be doing.

The team working on the project included not only staff from The Message but also volunteers who gave their time and expertise generously to help us. They included everyone from designers, computer experts and graphic artists to sheet-metal workers. Everyone's skills were needed, because it was a massive project – it took us around six months to get the bus fully fitted out.

Upstairs we had a massive TV screen, so that it looked like a cinema, with big Bosch speakers and some smaller screens at the back. Below the main screen was a metal rack holding DVDs, CDs and mini-disc players. Downstairs we had X-boxes, Playstations and more plasma screens, and a massive sound system. We also put in a large generator (we started with two small ones but they kept overheating, so we replaced them), a kettle, a microwave, a small office, drinks machines, security cameras, and plenty of storage space. We didn't have anything that could just be picked up and taken away, because we didn't want to get into any difficulties with theft.

We also had to plan how we were going to use the bus once we had it. Andy's original idea had been that we should use the bus to support the work of the Eden teams. On Friday nights we would drive down to one of the team areas, such as Openshaw or Wythenshawe, and meet up with the team. We would pray together about the evening's work, and then we'd open the bus and let the young people on. It was a great contact point for meeting them. Before we took the bus to a new area I would go out with the local Eden team members to get the views of the young people, and I always made contact with the police and local council too.

We did schools work as well, going into schools during the day and plugging the presence of the bus in their area that evening. I used to stand up in the lesson and say, 'Hi, I'm John and I'm a Christian.' Quite often I'd get the reply, 'You don't look like a Christian,' and that would open up a discussion. 'What does a Christian look like? Does it matter what you look like? Does God care what you look like?' They generally got quite involved in talking to me and were keen to see more of what we were offering. One of the gifts God has given me is the ability to relate to young people from all walks of life. As a result, there was always a crowd of youngsters waiting for us when the bus pulled in.

It all added up to a lot of work. I would be working at The Message five days a week, plus the evenings I was driving the bus, and occasionally other times. I was handling the admin associated with the bus; preparing talks, visiting churches and getting other people fired up about the potential of this direct ministry to young people; training the teams in all the issues connected with youth work (from handling aggressive behaviour to child protection law); visiting schools; and then taking the bus project out on the streets.

Gillian was working hard, too. The numbers in the church were small, so in the beginning there was much less pastoral work than there is now. On the other hand, she wanted to focus on evangelism and to enable the church to grow, so some changes were going to be needed. About a year after we had settled in at our new church, while she was still grappling with the problem of moving the church forward, she went on a retreat. As she was praying for the church family, she felt that she had a clear word from God, telling her how she could fulfil both parts of her vision for them. She was to retain their beloved traditional service, but to hold it at 9 a.m. on a Sunday morning. Then she was to start a new, informal 'seeker' service at 10.30, which would become the main service. This would be designed for people who weren't used to coming to church, and would have plenty of variety and interest, with modern music and an approachable style.

Obediently, she put this plan into action, and together we entered a difficult time of change. A few people didn't like the new arrangements, and a couple of folk left the church entirely. It was particularly painful for Gillian, because she came in for a lot of personal criticism for that – apparently driving away some of the few church members she had, who had been there for a long time. The numbers attending the early service declined, until at the lowest point there were only about three people coming to that service regularly. Other ministers might have given it up at that stage, but Gillian was sure that it was an important part of God's plan, so she persevered, and gradually the numbers picked up. As new people joined the church, some of them decided that they liked the quiet early service and chose that as the main focus for their worship.

All the same, it was a difficult time for us, and we found it emotionally quite stressful to know that so many of the congregation didn't like what we were doing. Gillian tried to explain that she wanted people to grow, and that she didn't believe that God had put her there simply to care for a tiny congregation, but we knew that behind our backs many people were complaining about all the changes. I found it particularly hard: I'd had so much rejection in the past that I was acutely sensitive to criticism. We had to accept that we couldn't please everyone all the time, because often what some people want from you is the direct opposite of what others want!

We were getting some stress from the pace of life, too. Gillian was fitting caring for the girls around her work as a vicar, while I had to work some weekends as part of my job. We have some very dear friends who help and counsel us, and it's always good to hear an objective view. Gillian's mentor Shirley was very helpful over this, and it was she who pointed out that although we were carefully prioritizing time for the girls, we also needed to make time for ourselves as a couple. Another day our friend Sue said to me, 'John, you've done ninety hours this week. What on earth do you think you're doing? Where does your family come in all this?' She was right to make me stop and think. It was time for another look at our diary, and time to try to cut back where we could. Our family is a gift from God, and a priority.

I found it difficult. When I'm working I get immersed in what we're doing, and in the lives of the young people we meet. I know how much difference we're making, and I want so much to help them and give them the chance to meet Jesus and know him as their Lord.

It's a constant juggling act, but Sue's advice was timely: 'It's God first, then your family, and then your work.' Even if the work is God's, we try to keep to that order, because although we have a responsibility to preach the gospel to the young people in Manchester, and to our church family, we have even more responsibility to teach and care for our own two lovely girls. We don't want them to grow up thinking that mummy and daddy had time for the church and not for them. So we try to programme in fun family time together, and to make sure that one of us is always there to tell them a bedtime story and put them to bed. With no family background of my own, building a Christian family is another thing I've had to learn from scratch.

Chapter 4　**A GOOD NIGHT OUT**

My job is pretty varied, but my main activity is running the Bus Ministry. A typical night out on the bus follows a pattern: we meet up with the team and pray for around half an hour; then we drive to the location where we'll be working and run the evening session for two to three hours; at the end we drive off, stop and have another prayer time and a debrief on the events of the evening; and then we drive the bus back to the garage and go home. However, 'typical' is never a word I'd use, because within that framework, every night is different.

When we meet up with the team for the area we're going to, we always have a chat about the local issues first. There may be some young people who have been barred from the bus (this happens occasionally if there are issues with aggression and violence), or particular events like gang fights or shootings that we need to be aware of. I allocate people to designated areas of the bus, four upstairs and four downstairs, with two people on the door, working always in mixed pairs, so there's always a male and a female together.

We also need to have our prayer time together, and hand over the whole evening to God. We do this first, before we drive to our location, so that we can do it in peace. Once, back in the early days, we parked up and sat down for our prayer time, even though there was already a group of youngsters waiting for us to open the doors. We finished praying and looked up to see, through the bus windows, a whole row of bare bums: the kids had got bored waiting and decided to moon at us! Other times we've been disturbed by kids shouting and swearing and sticking their fingers up at us, so we've learned to have our prayer time elsewhere, without disturbance.

Then we start up the generators, put the music on and open the doors. Generally the kids have seen the bus coming and they're already queuing up outside. Most of them are between the ages of nine and seventeen, though if we have too many to fit on the bus we sometimes split up the evening, and have the younger ones on at the start and the older ones later on.

After that, anything can happen! Some of them want to play with X-boxes and Playstations (although many of them have this stuff at home); we may show a film or play music. We're always careful if they bring their own DVDs or CDs, and check that they're appropriate, because we want to give out a consistent Christian message. Sometimes they play games, and often they just want to sit and talk with us and their friends – on a cold winter's night a warm, brightly lit bus is a better place to be than a dark street corner.

Our job is to be there for them, to engage with them and listen to them. We accept them as they are, because that's how God accepts them, but at the same time we have to make the bus a safe environment for everyone, so we have to have some ground-rules. We don't allow anyone on if they've been drinking too much or taking drugs – we monitor the kids carefully and can usually tell if they've had too much, and we have to make decisions on the spot. I've had young people smoking cannabis, and I've said to them, 'You're making it so obvious that you're taking drugs, and yet you want to come on the bus. Make up your mind which you want to do.'

If they're tooled up with a gun or a knife we ask them to leave – and we're prepared to restrain them if they kick off and have a go at any of the team. We make sure that everyone is fully trained to use minimum force to defend themselves. We've also had interesting incidents with BB guns being used to show off and scare people, but they can be as dangerous as real guns.

We have to take these precautions, but we do it unobtrusively, because we want the evening to be relaxed, so that the young people can meet the team and relate to each other. We have a great time playing games with some of the toughest cookies in the neighbourhood. If they come on wearing hoodies we get them to take the hood down. We don't have a problem with hoods but they hide your face, and on the bus we like the security cameras to pick up the faces – just in case.

Security cameras may sound a bit severe, but they're there for everyone's protection: if anything does go down (as it has on a number of occasions), we are able to produce the video evidence. For instance, one night a lad was told to leave the bus, and he accused the driver of hitting him and physically dragging him off the bus. The police happened to come by on a routine patrol, and he went over and told them he'd been assaulted. The police officer came back with him and spoke to me. 'We appreciate the work you're trying to do here,' she said. 'But if he's really been assaulted, you know I'll have to act accordingly.'

I was standing in the doorway of the bus, and I turned to the boy and said, 'OK, lad, I appreciate what you're saying. One of my team members will get into serious trouble if you continue with this allegation. You're entitled to do that. But I just want you to know that we've got the whole evening on video, so if you want to change your story, now would be a good time to do it.'

The boy looked over my shoulder and noticed the CCTV camera for the first time. We can't print what he said, but he decided that he didn't want to make the accusation.

It's hard to convey how volatile these situations can be. We see plenty of young people who behave fine and have no particular problems – they just want to have fun with their friends, and they'll have a laugh and a chat and enjoy being on the bus. But in these very deprived areas where crime rates are high, violence can be a way of life, and we have to be prepared. After seventeen years' experience in youth work, you get to know when something is about to kick off.

There was one lad who got really angry about something and smashed his fist through one of the plasma screens. I told him he was barred from the bus until he apologized. I never said anything about paying for the damage – they're huge things and very expensive, and I knew he could never afford to pay for it – but I wanted him to know that there had to be boundaries, and he had to be responsible for his actions. He just swore and said, 'I'm not doing that!' – so he's still barred. I'll allow him back if he apologizes and recognizes that he has done something wrong. It costs a lot of money to maintain our buses, and a lot of that is given prayerfully by people who don't have much themselves. We need to lead the young people to recognize that.

At the end of the evening we have the God Slot. We don't give anyone the choice of staying downstairs and continuing to play computer games or music, but they don't have to come to the God Slot, either: they can come upstairs and join in with the story and prayer time or they can leave the bus. We close down all the activities and say 'It's up or off!' We regularly have between thirty-five and sixty young people coming upstairs to join in.

First, one of the team will stand up and share their testimony. People often say to me, 'My testimony's not like yours, John,' and I say, 'I wouldn't want it to be. I wouldn't want you to have my past.' But everyone has a testimony, because it's the story of their encounter with God. When we let Christ into our lives, we're all equal.

The kids often start out with a bit of heckling, shouting and swearing, but once they've got over that, they realize that we've got something to share, and they love it. They love having the person in front of them, and they listen to the stories because they know they're true. At the end, they ask loads of questions.

We try to balance the questions with their prayer requests, and we get a lot of them. Kids will say, 'Will you pray for my auntie...or uncle...or friend.' Some of their requests are quite funny. We've had boys ask us to pray that they will get a girlfriend, 'and she has to look like this...' and they give us a detailed specification! Some of the requests are quite sad, but we take them all seriously. If a kid asks us to pray that they'll win the lottery, we say, 'God knows your heart. He knows what you really need. Do you really need to win the lottery?' If anyone really refuses to be serious, we ask them to leave, because it can be offensive when other people are talking about things that matter deeply to them. We often have eight or ten young people coming forward at the end for more prayer, or to talk seriously about whether they're ready to accept Christ into their lives.

If we have a kid who's swearing offensively about God, I sometimes say, 'I dare you to come forward and pray this prayer, because it takes a lot of courage. It takes a real man or woman to stand up and say, "Lord, I know I've done wrong and I want to give my life to you."' I don't have a problem with issuing a challenge like this: only the Holy Spirit knows what work he is doing in people's hearts, and we never know what life will hold for these young people. Sadly, some of those who used to come to our bus are no longer with us – they've died in different situations.

We always pray, 'Lord, please let your Holy Spirit work on this bus. We want to see miracles and we want to see lives being changed.' We have seen some amazing responses, and not just after months of work

– sometimes it's when we move into a new area. If God's going to do it, he will. We don't need to be there for six months before anything can happen. You never know what will make a difference to people, or what will enable them to open up sufficiently to admit their need for faith.

There was one group of youngsters from the Weaste project who were regulars on the bus, and they'd heard me talking about Lee Abbey. I said, 'Maybe we can go for a weekend away some time,' and they were really keen. A lot of these young people have never been out of Manchester, so a trip to Devon was exciting for them. Along with three helpers, I took twelve of them for a residential weekend, and a pretty wild time it turned out to be! We had to take alcohol off them before they got onto the bus, and even then they managed to smuggle about £100 worth of spirits in their luggage. They couldn't believe how far it was, and once we were out in the countryside they looked around in amazement. 'Where are the shops? Where are the pubs?' they kept asking, as if they couldn't believe that anyone could possibly live outside the city.

The journey took about eight hours. It would have been quicker if I hadn't had to pull over and stop so often, because they kept taking their seat belts off, messing about and throwing food. Their behaviour was pretty bad, considering we were doing something for their enjoyment. When we finally arrived at Lee Abbey we went to the Beacon Youth Centre and took them to their rooms. They were blown away by the place, and by the little chocolates and prayer cards left on their pillows to welcome them. It didn't make much difference to their behaviour, though.

We had a terrible time trying to get them up for breakfast. That was because they'd been up till about 4 a.m., smoking and drinking vodka. I challenged them that if they kept drinking they would have to leave, so they dutifully lined up and handed in their vodka bottles. The staff were impressed by their obedience, but I was suspicious when I noticed how wobbly they were. I opened the bottles and sniffed, and sure enough, they'd filled them with water. They'd emptied out the vodka by drinking it, and I was quite concerned about how fast they'd managed to dispose of it, but they didn't seem to suffer any ill effects.

The wild behaviour went on all weekend, as they were introduced to all sorts of 'adventure' activities. The archery was a popular option, but of course they weren't bothered about the targets, and I had my work cut out trying to stop them shooting each other. Then one evening, in the discussion session, a girl called Naomi from Lee Abbey gave her testimony. She came from a similar background to them, and she'd had similar issues with self-worth. The whole group seemed unusually quiet and subdued, and one or two of the girls had tears in their eyes. At the end of the session, as we stood up to leave, two of the young people went over and hugged her – not the sort of thing they would normally do. I felt it was a real breakthrough, and worth all the hard work and the nightmare of trying to keep them under some sort of control.

After that they kept asking if we could go away

again. I knew they'd seen something, and felt something, that they'd never met before: a level of caring and honesty that made them feel valued. Six months later one of these lads became a Christian on the bus.

Many of the young people we've worked with stay in my mind. Some of them have come through; they've gone into the army or the police, got a job, set up their own businesses, got married and settled down. Sadly, some of the others end up in prison and we go and visit them there. In *Nobody's Child* we printed a letter from Sara, who was sixteen when she was sent to prison for kidnapping and wounding. She said that she had written down 'some things about what it's like in here to try and stop kids from getting into trouble before it's too late...if you get the chance to, please read it to them because I don't want them to end up like me.' We kept in touch and I believe that God supported her through her sentence. Once someone has chosen to open the door to God, we see time after time how he never lets them go.

When we're chatting to the young people throughout the evening we're doing real youth work, gaining an insight into their lives, their worries and concerns, as they talk to us about anything from having a family to what they call 'religion'. The bus can be really buzzing with music and noise, but at the end of the night it's fantastic to hear them talking seriously about prayer without having to joke about it. When they've had real, honest interactions with people, they lose some of their defensive edginess because we've built up trust. They know the team members are real, ordinary, honest people who care about them.

There was one young girl who used to come along and always kick off about something, because there was so much anger in her. You could see from her eyes that she was really hurting inside, and it came out as aggression. She used to thump me on the shoulder and call me 'gayboy' and other names. Yet at the end of the night she would look at me pleadingly and say, 'You will come back next week, won't you?' In spite of all her aggression, she had picked up on the fact that the people on the bus cared about her.

That's why this work is so demanding: we have to be there for these young people, and often the most difficult ones are the most damaged ones who need our special care. I always say to our volunteers that they can't come along and take it easy. 'If you're too tired one night, just stay at home.' They have to be open and available and responsive, because you never know what baggage the kids are bringing in with them.

One night I was standing at the door of the bus and another of our regulars came up. She was a bright young girl, and she was usually quite loud and lairy, but she seemed a bit subdued.

I said, 'How are you?'

She said, 'Yeah, I'm all right.'

'No, really – how are you?'

'Well...not too good, really.'

I could have let it go, and I didn't want to push her, so I just said, 'Well, if you want to talk about it...'

Then she said quietly, 'Well, I came home tonight and my dad was hanging in the stairwell.'

She was trying to deal with her dad's suicide, and

if I hadn't made that extra effort to speak to her, I couldn't have given her that opening.

You never know what's going to happen, and you never know what the story will be. Often it's to do with loss – an illness, a shooting, a fight or a separation. Sometimes I just want to cry for them, because I can see what's missing in their lives. They long for love and security. If we listen to them, we can give them the space to offload some of their fear and loneliness in safe surroundings.

We take the buses to different areas of Manchester, where there are different teams of volunteers waiting for us, and we see the same quality of relationships being built up every time. Back at The Message we have a project called Genetik, where young people aged eighteen and over from different countries come to work with us. They spend time with The Tribe Academy doing music, they do schools work and prison work, and they join us on the bus. We use a lot of these guys when they're doing a six-month placement, where they live together in a house in an Eden team area. They're a great resource because they have passion, enthusiasm, energy and vision – and I add some training so that they are able to work on the streets with us.

There was one German girl whose English (fortunately) wasn't very good, and a guy went up to her on the bus and was being very aggressive, telling her what he'd like to do to her. I went up and told him he was out of order: 'We don't talk to you like that, so don't talk to a member of my staff like that.' I asked him to leave the bus. Karin asked me what he'd said, and I just said, 'He liked you – he liked you a lot.' That was all she needed to know. These young Christians have such a witness, they've put themselves on the front line for Jesus, and they're learning as they go along, but we have to protect them some of the time.

Teamwork is very important, and we have to support each other. It's quite a stressful and demanding situation to be in, and we're alert all the time. You're like a coiled spring, ready for anything, being aware of what's going on all around, and never letting your guard down. If a situation is starting to develop, we always give the young people a warning. 'Guys, please don't swear and shout.' The second time we say, 'If we have to tell you again you'll have to leave.' The third time we take action and they must leave the bus – and it's important that we follow through consistently, so everyone knows the score. It always works OK and I've never had a volunteer badly injured, even though there is sometimes some violence. We use a traffic-light response: green is OK, amber is a high alert, because there's the potential for something going down, and red is action stations, because something is happening.

We keep in touch using walkie-talkies rather than mobile phones, which are all locked away – you don't want to have anything on you that can be stolen – and we use a lot of sign language instead of saying things out loud. We monitor the whole bus closely all the time, with staff at the back, middle and front on both floors, keeping an eye on things. This isn't overkill. We work in some of the toughest areas of Greater Manchester, where drug-related crime and drive-by shootings are not just things you see in American cop movies – they're regular occurrences. We've had guys dealing drugs from their cars on the next street corner. Sometimes they have driven by and given us the 'gun' sign, because they want to get at the kids on the bus and deal stuff to them.

It's a privilege to work with the young people who live in these tough areas, not least because we know what a big effect we can have on their lives. The kids know we work in partnership with the police, so we aren't an escape from the law, but they know we don't repeat everything they tell us, apart from where we are bound by the law. The police support us (with finance as well) because they're so pleased with the response to our work. When we have up to 150 kids around the bus of an evening, the crime rate drops, because some of the young offenders are in the crowd listening to our music and not out nicking cars. The police also act with some sensitivity to make sure they don't break down the trust we're building up. If they want to arrest someone they won't do it on the bus, even if they know that's the best place to find them. They speak to them elsewhere.

It's important that we use the local teams who understand their areas and the sometimes volatile situations that can arise. Once we saw a nasty fight between two lads. One guy came from another patch and he hit a boy with a metal bar. The boy's dad came along and made the two boys fight it out. We pleaded with him and said, 'Why make them fight?' He replied, 'This is a tough area. If he doesn't stick up for himself he won't survive.' We had to try to understand his attitude – in a place where the culture was one of violence, he was trying to prepare his son for the reality of life as he saw it. We might be totally against violence, but we were going into their community and we needed to understand their culture and respect it. All we could do was pray that no one would get hurt.

At the end of the evening we wind up the God Slot with prayer, especially with any of the young people who have been affected by what's been said. Sometimes that effect is handed on to their family. They can have a little Gideon Bible, so their parents can see that we're not wacky Christians trying to brainwash their kids. One night a man sat at the back of the bus because he had come to collect his son, and he was in tears at the end of the God Slot. He came and asked us to pray with him, too.

We've had kids who used to come along to the bus and cause trouble, but now they prepare something for the God Slot and make their own contribution. They will stand up and lead a discussion about how they think God relates to us and speaks to us – it's a big achievement for them to stand up in front of 100 kids and talk like that.

We had one girl who used to come on the bus swearing and arguing with everyone, but gradually she settled down and seemed to appreciate the quiet time at the end of the evening. We gave her a copy of *Nobody's Child*, and she told us that after she'd read it she gave it to her mum, who read it and then passed it on to her uncle. Nowadays this girl behaves quite differently – she's a warm, gentle, respectful person. She brings her mates along to the God Slot and makes a thoughtful contribution.

She's an example of someone gradually inching her way towards faith, and we have quite a few in every area like that. They feel safe enough to join in with the God Slot, and they are actually ministering to others, though they may not themselves have ever stood up and prayed the prayer of acceptance. Maybe it's only later that they will understand their faith properly, but we meet them where they are today, and help them to explore their faith level as it is now.

On the other hand, we have youngsters who understand what we're offering, and show how hungry they are for understanding. In one of our areas there's a vicar who's been doing a lot of work with a group of kids aged eight to twelve. His church is full of activity, and as well as groups for Mums and Toddlers they run after-school clubs and give the kids a safe place to play football. The young people often have behavioural problems – they swear and spit in your face – and it takes a great deal of patience to work with them. A lot of it is learned behaviour: they shout because they're shouted at at home.

In these situations you have to be aware of the culture they're coming from. If you say to these kids, 'I love you and care about you', they'll say, 'He's a pervert' or 'He's gay'. Often there are very few men in their community, and they look up to inappropriate male role models: fighters and drug dealers. That vicar is doing fantastic work with the kids, giving them the sort of tough love that helps them, caring for them but setting boundaries for acceptable behaviour. He knows them all well, and understands what's going on in their lives.

I met one of 'his' kids one day when the bus was open for a fun day. He was a stocky little lad with a cheerful personality, but a bit of a loner with few friends. He looked round the bus and came up to me and said, 'Where's the bus going to be tomorrow?' I told him, and gave him one of the cards we give out, with a picture of the buses and the bus schedule on them. I gave him a card for 'Monday' saying where the bus would be, and he duly turned up for the whole session. At the end, after the God Slot, he said, 'So where will you be tomorrow, then?' So we gave him a card for Tuesday.

Sure enough, he turned up again, and for the whole week he followed the bus round, each day getting a card for the next day's location. At the end of the week he met one of the bus team in the street, stopped him and said, 'I want to be a Christian – how do I do it?' They stood and prayed together on the street corner, with people walking past, and afterwards the lad was really proud of himself. He was actually swaggering and saying, 'Well, I've done it now! I'm a Christian!' He knew what he wanted – even at the age of eleven – and he made sure he got it.

At the end of the prayer time we get all the kids off the bus and close the doors. If there are a lot of kids in the area we have to be very diligent and try to disperse them: sometimes when we pull away we've had young people lie down in front of the bus, or try to hang onto the back. We can't monitor the area after we've gone, but we try to leave a location knowing that the young people have gone, too, and not leave a problem behind us for the residents.

Tired as we are, often we're rejoicing as we drive away. We've seen amazing miracles on the bus, with young people getting to know Jesus. Every week we see at least one person give their life to Christ, and the challenge then is what we do next. The bus isn't a church, and the new Christians need a church that can meet them as we have – where they are, even if that means with a can of beer in one hand and a fag in the other. God can deal with that, but can the congregation? Not every church is geared up to work with young people who aren't used to sitting through a sermon and may be popping out every five minutes for a cigarette. That's where the Eden teams come into their own, because they are already linked with churches who are committed to this work, and are willing to embark on the long process of discipling these needy youngsters.

Meanwhile, we drive off for our time of prayer, then drop off the team members at their cars before the bus driver takes the bus back to The Message. A typical night? I suppose so. Yet every night is different, and everyone we meet is an individual, and only God is always the same, meeting us all where we are, and encouraging us to move on to something better.

Chapter 5

THERE'LL BE ANOTHER ONE ALONG IN A MINUTE!

A **round two and a half million** people live in Greater Manchester. About half a million of these are young people under the age of eighteen, many of them living in neglected inner-city areas. These are the communities which suffer from high crime, poor health, low educational achievement, a dilapidated environment, broken families and few opportunities. The vast majority of the population knows nothing about the love which God showed for the world through Jesus, and most of them have no interest in religion or traditional church services.

What drew me to The Message was its desire to help the kind of young people I care most about – the lost, deprived ones, who drift into drink, drugs and crime because they can't see anything else to do; those who are rejected like I was, and who feel unloved. Andy Hawthorne had a vision to see young people come to know Jesus, because he knew from personal experience that becoming a Christian transforms lives. I was a good example of that. If God hadn't intervened in my life, I'm pretty sure I wouldn't be here today. I'd have died on the streets through illness or violence or just giving up in despair.

The Message believes that when young people's lives are transformed, their communities can be restored, so by reaching out to the young people of Manchester, it's offering hope and a lifeline to the whole city. Maybe that sounds like a big claim, yet you can see evidence of it all around. A gang of rowdy youths can change the atmosphere of an area. Once vandalism and graffiti and petty crime become more frequent, everyone starts to feel threatened. That sets the stage for gangs to develop, kids start carrying weapons to defend themselves, and maybe the drug dealers move in. By the same token, if some of those key youngsters have somewhere to go, instead of hanging out on street corners; if they stop being bored and start to develop other interests; most of all, if they meet Jesus and let him turn their lives around, then that, too, is infectious. The mood of a whole estate can begin to change.

This was what we saw in the summer of 2000, when Soul Survivor moved up to Manchester. Soul Survivor's core values had always been teaching, worship and ministry, but Mike Pilavachi came to see the work of The Message and realized that they had to add evangelism, the missing dynamic. 'Unless we raise up worshippers,' he said, 'we're not really worshipping.' He decided to cancel Soul Survivor 2000, and moved the entire event to Manchester for ten days of mission. That summer 11,000 people from twenty nations went out into the city, to preach the gospel in word and deed.

That in itself was a staggering achievement, but one particular event really demonstrated what could be done. A policeman called Phil Green had been working on the Swinton Valley Estate, a deprived area with a high crime rate, boarded-up houses, and litter and mess everywhere. He came up with the idea of bringing in a thousand young people to clean the whole place up, clear gardens, do up the Community Centre, and put in a park. All the young people they made contact with on the estate were invited to huge free parties in the Evening News Arena. They worked hard, and the effect was amazing.

For a start, you couldn't move for Christians – young, enthusiastic Christians – and everyone was talking about Jesus. Suddenly it was quite normal to hear people talking about God. Then, the physical changes they brought about were striking: once the place had been cleaned up, it looked completely different. All the residents got involved, and people started to take a pride in their area. The biggest change, though, no one could have predicted. The previous weekend on that estate there had been eleven burglaries and any amount of car crime. During the whole ten days of the mission there were no recorded incidents of crime at all, and in the following months, the police recorded a sustained reduction in crime of 45 per cent.

No one gets involved in outreach work with the aim of reducing crime, but when it happens, it catches the attention of people who wouldn't normally take much interest in the church. The police and the press started to take notice. People began to wonder what made young people give up their time to try to bring help and hope to these communities. For us at The Message, it supported our belief that the way to help was to make reaching the young people our top priority.

That short ten-day mission was unusual. The key to the normal Eden work was something different: sustained, long-term effort. To make a real difference to the lives of the most broken, hurting and hopeless people, you have to be there with them. The Eden Teams make a bold statement by moving into those estates permanently. When people ask them, 'Why have you moved here?' they tell them the truth – they want to help and support the community, because that's what God is telling them to do. They have made a long-term commitment to that neighbourhood. Relationships get established, friendships are built and faith is shared. It's the best possible kind of witness.

It was a privilege to run the Eden Bus Ministry, and to support the guys who have lived and worked in these areas for years, getting to know the young people and their families. We could come in and offer them a safe place to meet, a range of activities and an opportunity to talk about what matters to them. By 2001 there were five Eden Teams in operation, in Salford, Openshaw, Longsight, Swinton and Harpurhey. We were out several nights a week visiting different areas. In fact, we were beginning to struggle – the bus was always in demand, and although we took care to keep it in good condition, from time to time we would have a breakdown, and that would mean letting people down. It was clear that the work couldn't expand much further without a second bus. Having been involved in fitting out the first one, I knew what was involved. The financial implications of the idea were staggering, and we only knew one way to get that sort of money – through prayer. We didn't tell anyone what we were hoping for, we just put it to God. If it was his will for the work to expand, he would show us the way.

One afternoon we were out on the bus in the Weaste area of Salford, and John and Rose Lancaster had come down to see how the work was progressing. Rose was waiting for an operation on her hip, and she was in quite a lot of pain, but she wasn't going to let that stop her visiting us. John and Rose support several charities, and run a medical mission overseas, but they are great believers in what they call 'the ministry of relationships'. They don't believe in just giving money to support causes, because money alone doesn't show people the love of Jesus. All Jesus' ministry was about bringing people to God, and so theirs is a two-fold ministry: meeting needs but also making relationships. They are very active partners in all the work they support, visiting and getting to know the people involved, and encouraging our volunteers with their cheerful friendliness and their down-to-earth understanding of the work we're doing.

This particular afternoon Rose was standing on the pavement as I was talking to a couple of girls in the bus doorway. Just then a lad came along the street on his bike, swerved towards the bus, wobbled a bit and crashed into Rose – and his handlebars struck her on the hip that she was having trouble with. She went white with the pain, and I could see her biting back the tears. She told me afterwards that she wanted to scream as the pain shot down her leg. She grabbed onto the bus door, and after a bit we helped her to climb inside and sit down.

When I got a quiet moment I went in and sat down with her.

'I'm really sorry about that,' I said. 'The lad was really sorry, too – he even apologized!'

'That's all right, John,' she said. 'It's a bit better now – but it got me thinking. I mean, I've got a problem with my hip, but I can get treatment for that, and once I've had my op I'll be OK. I'm in pain at the moment, but it's only temporary. But I've listened to some of these kids' stories, and they're in pain in their whole lives. I heard you talking to those girls – you're so caring, and that's what they need, people to care for them. I could have cried about my hip, but I could cry even more for these kids.

'We've had a bit of a chat, and we think your work's so valuable. Would you like the money for another bus, so you can do more?'

I was staggered. We hadn't mentioned a second bus to anyone – except God, in our regular prayer times. I couldn't believe they could be offering us the whole thing on a plate – especially after their incredible generosity in buying us the first one.

I told them what we'd been praying for. 'Well,' said Rose comfortably, 'sometimes God just gives you a nudge. Sometimes quite hard,' she added, rubbing her hip.

We started looking for another bus at once. It was important that it had a reliable engine as well as sound bodywork. You can build any amount of equipment into a nice-looking bus, but it's no good if the engine dies and it lets you down. I looked in magazines and talked to everyone I knew, hoping someone would hear of something suitable. Then I found an advert for a coach which had once been the Nottingham Forest Football Club tour bus. It looked perfect, and it would be great for long journeys like going to Soul Survivor.

I went to meet the owner, but he wanted £64,000. The price was understandable – the whole thing was kitted out for touring, with seats, tables, a separate unit with showers, and even a bar on the top deck. His price took account of all the fittings, and of course he wasn't to know that we would be ripping them all out and starting again. I offered him £26,000, but he turned me down. 'I might as well give it away,' he said.

I was disappointed, because I'd felt so sure that it was the right bus for us, but I went away and started looking again. The weeks went by, and I didn't find anything to match that first bus. Then, three months later, I got a phone call from the owner. He hadn't managed to sell it, and he was prepared to lower his price. In the end I bought it for my original amount I offered! I drove it back to The Message, feeling increasingly pleased with my bargain. The bus had an automatic Mercedes Benz engine, and was fantastic to drive. Then I got down to the hard work of planning once again.

I sat down with a good friend who works in accounts and we went through everything we would need – the plasma screen, the X-boxes and Playstations, the seating arrangements, even the mobile phones. It was a new experience for me – I had to draw up a budget for about £80,000, and I was a bit nervous when I presented it to John Lancaster. I thought I'd allowed for everything, but John, who is a wise and experienced businessman as well as one of the most generous people I know, looked thoughtful.

'That's fine,' he said. 'But I think we'd better allow a bit extra for contingencies – in case things turn out a bit more expensive than you think.' Bless him, he was right, and we needed the extra. I so appreciated not having to go back to him to ask for a bit more, each time something turned out to cost more than I'd budgeted for.

We made detailed plans. The second bus was going to be different in minor ways from the first: for instance, the location of the generator was changed to make it more vandal-proof. We'd learned some useful lessons from our experience of running Eden Bus 1.

By this time The Message had moved from our cramped quarters in Cheadle to a big office building on an industrial estate. The offices were new and well equipped, and we had room for both of the buses to be parked on our own premises and under cover. I had to learn more about project management, and make sure that every bit of the fitting-out job was done properly and in the right order. It was a real learning curve for me. In the end we had a second fantastic vehicle, fully equipped and professionally spray-painted with our logo and some great graphic design.

We had a big launch party, with the Tribe performing and both buses open for viewing. Everyone was pleased with the end result. The kids climbed on and said 'Wow – it's really cool!' We always have the best and latest technology, not just to impress them, but because they need to see excellence. It makes them feel valued that we are prepared to offer them an environment of this standard. If we can care like this, it's easier to tell them that God loves them, too. Whenever the kids say that the bus is fantastic, I say, 'If you think this is good, think how much more amazing God is.' It was a very exciting time. We were ready to go up a gear with the Bus Ministry.

For one thing, a second bus enabled us to go into schools more often. The Message already had a ministry to schools, doing assemblies and RE lessons, and sometimes running short missions. The bus gave an added dimension. On one recent mission we took the bus along and all the RE lessons that week were conducted on the bus. We did talks on citizenship and self-worth, with lots of quizzes and interactive activities. For instance, we show the kids two pairs of jeans – one comes from Oxfam and costs £2, while the other has an expensive designer label. 'Which one is worth more?' we ask. 'What about the person wearing them – are people worth more because of the clothes they wear?' We show them pictures of well-known faces and ask who is the most valued – David Beckham or Mother Theresa? We do presentations, group work, games and discussion. The students enjoy it because it's something different, in a different environment, and the teachers enjoy it because they can have a lesson off, sit at the back of the bus with a cup of coffee, and catch up on their marking!

Usually we encourage the students to go to the big concert at the end of the week, where there will be a proper presentation of the gospel and an invitation to respond, but on this occasion I just had a feeling that the time was right. I knew that the teacher wasn't a Christian – these days RE is about teaching five major world religions, not about Christianity alone, and teachers do not necessarily have a faith of their own, even if they are RE specialists. I didn't want to offend her, but at the end of the lesson I decided to ask the young people if they wanted Jesus to come into their lives. We had a big class of about forty-five pupils, and to our amazement, twenty-seven kids put up their hands. We gave each of them a Gideon Bible and encouraged them to go to the concert that evening led by Blush, The Message's girl band. I made sure that the Christian teachers in the school followed up that amazing response.

Of course, having another bus meant more work. I was already at full stretch, managing the organization, fund-raising, giving talks, driving the first bus, and even cleaning it. I didn't mind what I did, but I couldn't put in any more hours than I already did, and anyway, I couldn't be in two places at once. We needed more staff. I needed team leaders for each area as well as a mechanic to keep the buses on the road.

Recruiting staff for the Bus Ministry wasn't just a simple matter of advertising for them. We needed people who really cared about the work. You could have the most fantastic bus in the world – it could have a swimming pool on the roof! – but if the staff don't share the vision, it won't work. I often get letters

As a child I wondered why I didn't have a mum and dad like other kids, and why no one in my family ever wanted to contact me.

Lee Abbey was the place where Gillian and I met, and where a good deal of my healing and growing took place.

Later I took groups of young people to the Beacon Youth Centre for their first experience of life outside Manchester.

The Robinson family: John, Gillian, Natalie and Leah

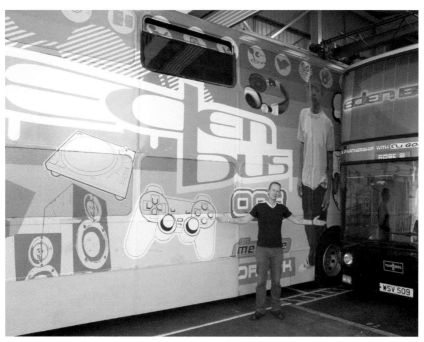

The Bus Ministry: Eden Bus 1: Rose Lancaster's birthday present!

Every night on the bus is different, as young people come to have fun, meet their friends, and talk to the volunteers about the things that matter to them.

Paul and I rode 240km in blistering temperatures to raise funds for The Message.

Speaking in a church with no walls, on the other side of the world – yet I felt very close to these people who live on the margins of society.

The Tribe reached young people by singing about God in language everyone could understand – with music they loved.

Manchester is a thriving city – yet it has run-down areas of high unemployment and high crime. The Eden Teams live and work in these communities.

David Cameron, the Conservative party leader, came to see the bus ministry for himself.

It was a huge surprise when I received the Unsung Hero award for our work on the bus ministry. Linda Robson, centre, was a true star and read out some of my story.

from people saying that they'd like to have a similar bus in their area, but I always tell them the same thing. The key ingredient isn't the equipment or the facilities: it's the Holy Spirit inspiring people with the vision, enthusiasm and commitment for the work.

For instance, you need about forty volunteers. That's because we always have a team of at least eight on the bus at any one time, and as these people have jobs and lives and they need some evenings free, there needs to be a rota. They take it in turns to go out. Even if the bus breaks down and can't go out, those volunteers will still turn up to talk to the kids, at the time and place where the bus would have been. These kids are let down so often, it's really important that they see our faithfulness and commitment to them in this. When the volunteers turn up, it shows that they care for them. We get some strange looks sometimes, when the team is standing there in the pouring rain with hands on each other's shoulders, praying together before a session just as we would if we were on the bus. Sometimes those evenings turn out to be the most effective, because the young people have seen how committed we are as individuals.

By this time, we weren't just going into the Eden Project estates. The Bus Ministry had been recognized by the police, as its effectiveness in reducing crime, juvenile nuisance and anti-social behaviour was proved again and again. It wasn't unusual for the police to make a special request for us to target an area strategically, giving us funding from their crime prevention budget. We weren't going in as crime-busters, though. We never went into an area unless we had done thorough preparation and had the support of the local church to follow up our work.

Often the churches themselves would make the first contact, and ask us to come and give a presentation about the work and tell them how we could work in partnership. I was always realistic about the cost – both personal and financial – and I always explained first and foremost that what they needed was a team of local volunteers, on fire with the gospel and a vision for the work. They needed to go and talk to the young people in the area, and make sure that they thought a visit one night a week by a mobile youth centre would be a good idea. If they didn't want it, it wouldn't come to anything, because they'd just trash the bus. If they did want it, they'd take ownership of it, and then we could get something started.

Once we had the volunteers, there was still a lot to do. We had to get every volunteer police checked, because they would be working with young people. Then I had to train the bus drivers, and when they completed the course they got a certificate saying they were qualified to drive a bus of that size and weight. The drivers were vital, because the best people to take a bus into an area are the people who live there. The kids love it when they see their mums and dads driving our great big bus into their street.

The volunteers don't just have to be drivers – they have to have other gifts, too, because they have to operate as part of the team. Once they've parked up, they lock up the driver's area of the bus and get to work alongside everyone else. I give everyone training on handling aggression – not self-defence, but tips on

body language. To do this work you have to understand that you can be a Christian without being
treated like a total muppet. Some youths think that
because you're a Christian they can spit in your face
and swear, and you'll have to take it. With training,
people learn that they can be strong and set boundaries for acceptable behaviour without resorting to
physical contact.

We treat the young people with respect, but we
don't stand for anyone kicking off or spoiling the
event for others. Sometimes we have to ask people to
leave (for instance, if they're picking fights with other
kids or the staff, or if they're smoking or drinking),
but we generally manage to do it in a good-humoured
way.

There was one night when I made a big mistake. I
saw a young lad get onto the bus – where we have a
strict no-smoking policy – with a cigarette in his
hand, but he tucked it under his coat. I stopped him
and said, 'Mate, you're smoking.'

'No, I'm not,' he said.

'Well, you're on fire, then,' I said, ''cos there's smoke
coming out of your coat! Can't you read that sign?'

Straight away the lad started kicking off, shouting
and swearing and punching. I should have known better: I knew enough about dyslexia and other reading
difficulties. He couldn't read and he thought I was
taking the mickey out of him.

I did have to keep him off the bus that night, but
once we were outside I apologized to him. I told him
he was off the bus for smoking, but I wasn't going to
bar him for having a go at me, because I'd been in the

wrong, and I shouldn't have said what I said. We never had any trouble with him after that.

It's a good example of the kind of awareness we need. Some of our kids can't read or write, some come from difficult and violent home situations, and they bring all these sensitivities with them. It makes their behaviour very volatile, and we have to strike a balance: we need to understand them as individuals, but at the same time set firm boundaries for behaviour, so that the rules are the same for everyone. It's a way of making everyone feel secure.

Our volunteers are very special people, and many of them have their own amazing stories to tell. A good example is Kerry, who was introduced to me by one of my colleagues on the bus. He said that she wanted to help with the bus work, so we went along to meet her. She didn't need much prompting to share her testimony, and before long she was standing up in the God Slot and telling a crowd of young people, too. You could have heard a pin drop as she told her story.

Kerry had heard about God in lessons at school, and she asked her mum about him. 'Well, God's like a fairytale that some people believe in,' she said. 'A bit like Father Christmas.' Kerry thought that sounded a bit stupid, and decided she wasn't going to believe in God. She had a difficult home life, and grew up lacking in confidence. When Kerry was fifteen she suffered from severe depression and was admitted to a psychiatric hospital, where she was put on a complicated drug regime. What she didn't realize was that she could get addicted to some of these drugs, and before long she was resorting to all sorts of tricks to get more: lying to the nurses, stealing drugs or buying them from other patients.

When she was discharged she was sent to a Social Services hostel and managed to get a job, but she still needed to buy drugs. It wasn't easy to get hold of enough diazepam on the street, so she tried other things – cannabis at first, then heroin. She didn't like the hostel, but she wasn't earning enough to pay rent and buy drugs too, so she moved in with a drug dealer who lived in the same street. There she got into the terrible cycle of drug addiction: getting up in the morning and taking whizz or coke to get the energy to go out and score – and then buying more stuff to come back down.

Soon money became a real issue. At that time she scarcely realized the trouble she was getting into – her need for the drugs blotted everything else out. She transported drugs for the dealers she knew, and did some selling. She was mixing with some seriously hard guys, who found her innocent good looks useful. They would do burglaries and steal cash cards and chequebooks. Then they would get Kerry to fake signatures and spin the bank staff a story about having to get cash for her mum. They would make small withdrawals from a cash machine to check that an account was working OK, then send Kerry in to talk to the bank manager and explain that she needed to make a £6,000 withdrawal. She could hardly believe that they got away with it for so long, but she usually got the money. She handed it over and they would give her a small cut of the profits. Looking back, she described herself as naïve and desperate for money.

She was desperate for love, too, and she tried to find it by sleeping around, even prostitution, telling herself that if a man wanted to sleep with her it surely meant that he liked her – but realizing every time that it probably wasn't true. She was estranged from her family, and had no real friends – only people she did deals with. She ended up living rough on the streets.

One winter night she had climbed into the back of a smashed-up car to get out of the wind, but she was so cold that her body was numb. She felt lost and alone, and she knew she was literally freezing. She thought, 'This is the last time I'm going to feel anything.' She knew that if she went to sleep in those temperatures, she would die. She looked up at the sky and said, 'God, if you're out there, I've really messed up, and I'm sorry. I wish I could tell my family that I loved them. I know I could have done better and I know you probably won't want me, but this is it.' She said her prayer, closed her eyes and went to sleep, not expecting to wake up.

When she woke up the next morning she was surprised, but she didn't stop to think that God might have saved her. Life went on in the same way. She moved in with a boyfriend and got pregnant, and a couple of weeks later she got into a fight with a bus driver, and found herself running away from the police. Jumping on another bus to get away, she sat down next to a guy who seemed concerned about her.

'You look pretty freaked,' he said. 'Have you been smoking crack? I used to do drugs, but I'm a Christian now.'

'Oh, what a nutter!' she thought, but she liked the

feeling of someone taking an interest in her. A week or so later she bumped into another man from a church where she sometimes collected a food parcel. 'Here we go again,' she thought, as he started to tell her that Jesus loved her. Then one day she was watching her boyfriend playing basketball when a girl came and sat on the bench beside her. 'Why aren't you playing?' she asked.

'I'm pregnant,' Kerry replied. Usually at this point in the conversation the other person would say, 'When's the baby due?', but this girl said, 'Can I pray for you?'

'Oh, no,' Kerry thought, 'here's another one! My face must just attract you guys.' She had forgotten about her prayer, and it didn't occur to her until later that it was only after she had prayed for the first time that all these Christians kept popping up in her life.

Eventually she was persuaded to go on an Alpha course, and she enjoyed it. It made her happy to feel that someone was paying attention to her, but by now, she didn't really trust anyone because she had been used and let down so many times. She didn't know what a real friend was. She had split with her boyfriend, because once their son was born, Kerry wanted to sort her life out for his sake, but the boyfriend wasn't willing to give up his drugs. She met up with the Christians from time to time, and she really wanted to believe what they were telling her, that God cared for her and had better things in store for her. But somehow she couldn't bring herself to believe that anything in her life could change.

Then one day she was sitting in her kitchen while the baby was asleep. She recalls:

'I looked down and I could see this little ant crawling round on the floorboards. He was going round and round in circles, up and down, really busy, but he wasn't going anywhere. And I thought, "Well, I won't squash you, I'll put you out of the window."

'And I went and got a piece of paper and put it down in front of him, but he kept veering away. I was following him round with this piece of paper, trying to pick him up so he wouldn't get stomped on. I was talking to him and saying, "Look, the offer's in front of you – just climb on. I know I'm big and I know I'm scary and I know you don't know what I am, but just step on the paper and believe in me."

'And then he did – he crawled onto the paper, and I carried him over to the window and put him safely outside.

'And then I thought, "Hang on – that's what these Christians keep asking me to do, just step on and have faith in something I don't really understand."'

Kerry realized that she had tried to save herself and it hadn't worked. She'd tried every angle to make herself feel loved, and everything had ended in disaster. She thought, 'I really need to do this.' At that moment she knew that she believed, and that she had faith.

'As soon as I realized it, I felt as if a big weight had lifted off me. I was jumping around the room with excitement. I suddenly knew that I was worth something, I was special, and God cared about me enough to follow me round till I accepted him.'

Kerry had a hard struggle after that, because she had learned all the habits of being rejected and thinking she was worthless, but gradually she got stronger. 'I realized I didn't have to go to extreme lengths to be loved – I could just be me.'

These days she has a new confidence – confidence enough to stand up on the bus and tell her story. All her rage and bitterness has gone, and in its place she finds she has love in her heart, which she wants to share. 'I want people to feel the happiness I feel – specially that moment when I realized I was worth more, and I jumped around my kitchen with joy! I've learned to love myself, and I've learned to love and respect other people, too.'

Kerry is just one of our bus helpers, an ordinary single mum living on a tough estate. But she is a wonderful person, and hers is an amazing story of how a life can be changed by an amazing God.

Chapter 6

UNLOCKING THE DOOR

As I worked on the bus and got to know the various areas of Manchester better and better, I was also getting to know more about the work that The Message was doing. Over the years the projects evolved and changed – not just the bands and the Eden Projects, but other ideas which were developed to meet specific needs. There's Life Centre, a youth café where young people can find a whole range of things, from training and IT resources to counselling services and sports and leisure activities. The Big Deal is a wide-ranging community project which sets up small events in different areas – like The Big Bike Ride, The Big Teacup and so on. It contacts different organizations such as the police, the local council and the churches, and gets them working together and cooperating. The small one-off events usually generate much more long-lasting relationships and ongoing work. Genetik is another initiative that offers opportunities for people to get involved with its music ministry, evangelism and discipleship training. All these projects came out of The Message Trust's concern for reaching every young person in Manchester, meeting their needs and talking to them about God in language they could understand.

I was specially interested in Reflex, the prison work that was being rolled out across Young Offender Institutions across the north-west. The idea was to put a team into each institution, working in partnership with other Christian agencies. The volunteers would befriend the young offenders while they were still inside, and be ready to offer them help when they were released, finding them work and places to live and linking them with local churches and Eden Project teams. I knew how badly that was needed.

I was fourteen when I was locked up for the first time, sentenced to six weeks in a detention centre for arson. It was a terrible shock: I honestly believed the fire was an accident. I'll never forget that sound of doors being slammed and keys being turned in the lock. During the day we were kept busy cooking in the kitchen, washing floors and cleaning the toilets. The days were hard, but the nights were terrible. We slept in dormitories, and the bully boys would come and roll you up in a blanket and give you a beating. If you made any noise they used to put a sock in your mouth and tie it there. The staff must have known what was happening, but they didn't do anything. I think the place was easier to run if there was a pecking order established among the boys.

When I was seventeen I was arrested for burglary, and spent five weeks in the local remand centre. It was another grim place, filled with young men who lived violent lives, and there were plenty of fights and beatings. That was where I was so depressed that I tried to commit suicide. I couldn't see any way of breaking out of a hopeless life. I couldn't break away from the gang I hung out with, because I had no job, no home and no money. I thought, 'This is all there is to life: running with a gang of people I'm afraid of, or getting locked up in a prison cell. I've got no future and no hope.' I stole an aluminium ashtray from the staffroom when I was cleaning it, and that night in my cell I bent the metal until it tore in two. Then I used the jagged edges to slit my wrists. The result was that I made my life even worse than it had been: my injuries were stitched up in the prison medical unit, then I was put in a straitjacket and placed in a solitary cell.

Eventually my case came to court and I was sentenced to eighteen months in borstal – the forerunner of today's Young Offender Institutions. Once again there was a strict regime of work and fitness training, but this time I was put into a single cell. It had a bed, a sink and a toilet, and I suppose the good thing was that no one could get in to beat you up at night – though by then I had learned to handle myself, and I could (and did) fight with the toughest. Those nights were long and lonely, though, and I had plenty of time to think. I promised myself that I would never do anything to get banged up in prison ever again. How could I have been so stupid? Yet when I was released, I didn't have the first idea of how to make a decent life for myself. I bumped into a few of my old mates, went for a drink with them, and slipped back into the same old ways.

Part of the problem was the lack of support. I'd had no real experience of life, and I didn't know how to apply for a job or even how to go about finding help with housing. I'd been offered a place in a hostel, but it sounded too much like the prison I'd just left, and anyway I didn't know anyone there. At least back on the streets I had my old mates, a few familiar faces. I couldn't get a job: no one would take me on when they knew I was homeless and had been in borstal. It was a vicious circle: no money meant I couldn't find a place to live. No home meant I couldn't give an address to an employer, so I couldn't get a job. No job meant no money...and so it went round. It wasn't until I met Tony and his wife Sylvia – the wonderful Christian couple who took me in, let me share their home and gave me work to do – that I was able, for the first time, to learn how to live a normal life. Having work and earning some money gave me some self-esteem, something else that I lacked.

I knew from first-hand experience what kind of life led young people into prison in the first place; I knew how terrible prison life could be for them; and I knew how badly they needed support if they were ever going to stay out of prison and make a new start. The Reflex project is a brilliant idea, and it was triggered by the realization that if the mission of The Message is to reach all the young people in Greater Manchester, then surely the young people in Young Offender Institutions are among the most needy and hopeless of all. Suicide rates in these prisons are at a record level, such is the despair felt by those young inmates. Their one hope and chance of breaking free from the destructive lives they are living is the freedom and purpose that only Jesus can bring. If we can reach them with that message of hope, and back it up by the practical love and help they need, then there is a great work to be done for God.

I had thought for a long time that my experience of prison meant that one day God would want me to work for him there. In fact, I had already had one brush with employment in the prison system, which hadn't worked out too well. When Gillian and I were first thinking about moving on from Southampton, I saw a job advertised for an assistant chaplain in a Young Offender Institution in Market Drayton, and I applied and was interviewed. The interview went well, and as I left I heard the chaplain say, 'Yes! He's just what we're looking for!' It was a great boost to my self-confidence when I received the formal offer of a job, but only a few days later I had a phone call from the prison governor, saying that he didn't want me after all. I couldn't understand it, as everyone there had known all about my previous convictions and everything about me – I had been completely honest and hadn't held anything back. I was offended that the post could be snatched away from me after I'd been offered it on my own merits, because I was the best man for the job.

I wrote to Jack Straw (then Home Secretary) saying how wrong it was to interview someone and offer a job, and then retract the offer. By then I was deeply confused: was this job part of God's will for us or not? I prayed about it and came to the conclusion that God's answer was 'Not yet' for prison work. Two weeks later I got another letter reinstating the original job offer, but by then I had already accepted my job with The Message. All the same, I praised God and thanked him for the experience, because the whole thing had been good for me. It had showed me that I was good enough for that work, and that I could be valued for who I was and because of the experiences of my past life, not just in spite of them.

So when I started looking closely at the possibility of working with the Reflex project, I thought that perhaps this was to be my way into prison work. Maybe now the time was right. The job as Prison Team Leader looked interesting: after a couple of years of working on the Bus Ministry, I knew several young people currently in local Young Offender Institutions, some of them the elder brothers of kids who came regularly to the buses. It would be good to be part of the team that offered help and hope to them. All the same, it would be hard to give up the Bus Ministry, which I loved, and who would take over from me?

As so often happens, the right man came along at just the right time. Steve had moved up from the south of England, like us, and he was a gifted youth worker. As soon as I met him I knew he would be able to handle all the complex aspects of the Bus Ministry, so I felt more than happy to hand over to him. In fact, he had plenty of work to do: we'd had several attacks on the buses, and one night there was a serious fire on Eden Bus 2. Miraculously, that night the bus hadn't been parked under cover, where it usually was, but in the yard. This not only saved the shed from burning down, but also meant that Eden Bus 1 wasn't harmed. Even so, there was a lot of repair work to be planned, paid for and coordinated, and it kept Steve pretty busy for a while.

Meanwhile, I became part of the chaplaincy team in the four Young Offender Institutions in and around Greater Manchester. I knew it was a privilege, and I believed that it was God's will for me, yet I can't describe my feelings when I made my first visit, and I heard that characteristic sound of the doors slamming behind me, and the jingle of the keys on the prison officer's chain as he unlocked and locked every door we went through. You might have heard that sound on television programmes, even in comedies like Ronnie Barker's *Porridge*, but it doesn't convey the dread that you feel when it happens for real.

Real prisons aren't filled with cheeky lovable rogues like Norman Stanley Fletcher, engaged in humorous banter and mischievous battles of wits with comic prison officers. They're filled with desperate, hurting, rejected people, who long to be free, but who, through circumstances and their own bad choices, are stuck in a cycle of destruction. I knew it because I had once been one of them. As soon as the first door slammed behind me I felt as if I'd made a leap back in time through twenty years to my youth – to being shut in to serve a sentence that seemed to go on for ever. I followed the prison officer through the corridors to the landing where I was going to work, trying to look cool, calm and collected, but in fact I was sweating and shaking.

When *Nobody's Child* was published, lots of people read the book, and I started getting even more invitations to speak in prisons as well as in churches and at Christian events. So I'd visited prisons and Young Offender Institutions lots of times, and every time I'd found those first few minutes scary, but those were only flying visits. I knew I would go in, meet the chaplain, go down to the chapel or the gym where I was speaking, deliver my talk, maybe chat to a few prisoners, and then I'd be out again, all within a couple of hours. This time it was different. This was going to be my working environment: I was going to have to come here every day, and go through the door-slamming and key-jangling over and over again. I wondered how long it would take for me to get used to it.

One of the hardest things was being locked on a landing for a whole evening, knowing that I couldn't just turn and walk away when I wanted. For those few hours, I was as much a prisoner as the young men I was talking to, and even though I was there voluntarily, I still found it nerve-racking. I got over my initial feelings of panic, but I still had to deal with being back 'inside'.

Every time I think I've arrived at a stable place where the past can't hurt me any more, I get into some situation like this and find that I'm not as strong as I thought I was. Sometimes it's surroundings like these that bring back memories I'd rather not have – I want to lock them away and forget them. Sometimes it's the young people talking about their lives – being let down and rejected, feeling like scum because they've allowed themselves to be sucked into crime or drink or drugs. I know what that feels like, and it brings back all the times when I felt completely worthless. It stirs up feelings inside me, and I know that I haven't left them behind completely yet.

I believe that God is still dealing with the damage

in my life and is still in the process of healing me. I think of it like a bottle of fizzy lemonade: if you take the top off all at once, it fizzes up and spills over and makes a terrible mess. If I had to face up to all the hurt and rejection and pain and anger at once, I couldn't cope. Instead, he's letting in the air little by little, letting the pressure off and calming the turmoil that's hidden inside. It's a gradual healing, and though perhaps I'd like it all to be over and done with, I know that his way is thorough and, in the end, it is the best.

It's like thinking about being in God's presence. We couldn't handle being exposed to his holiness and purity, so he gives us little tastes and glimpses of himself, to prepare us and help us to understand him more and more as time goes by. I trust in his healing, and I believe it will one day be complete in all of us. There have been many times when I've walked away from a prison after listening to some young guys telling me their stories, and I have cried to God and asked him to work in their lives the way he has in mine.

Sometimes I've been talking to the toughest young people, who have already been through so much pain and trouble in their lives, and I've said, 'Do you know that God cares about you? If not, I can tell you I'm a hundred and ten per cent sure that he loves you and wants your life to be so much different. And I know that because of what God has done in my life.' Lots of them say, 'I can so relate to your story!' Lots of them grew up in care, too, and they've all fallen into crime for one reason or another. They look at my tattoos and my scars, and they start asking how God changed my life.

I've learned something really important – that all those terrible experiences weren't just a horrible mistake. Those memories are not a meaningless part of my life that I should reject and lock away and throw away the key – even though I'd like to, because it's so painful to recall those dark times. I believe the devil tried to destroy me in the past, through rejection, through loneliness, through violence and danger. But God wants to use me. He takes the things that the devil tried to destroy me with, and he turns them into tools that he can use. The pain and destruction of my past make the bridge between me and young people in similar circumstances, so I can relate to them and do his work of reaching out to them. I can stand up covered in tattoos and scars and say, 'Look what God has done in my life.' My past can be used for God.

When I spent an evening on the landings, I was usually just talking to the lads. Some of them were on remand, waiting for their case to come to court, so they knew that soon they would either be sentenced or released. It made them nervous and edgy, especially as the court date approached. Even when they were pretty sure they'd get a custodial sentence, they were always tormented by a shred of hope that they might get a community sentence and be released. The lads who had already been sentenced were a bit more laid back: they knew how long they'd got to serve, and they generally had a lot of time on their hands. They liked to sit down and talk to me about their lives. None of them wanted to come back to prison, ever, but many of them had a shrewd idea of how hard it might be to make a new start when they got out. One or two of them had read *Nobody's Child*, and they looked at me and said, 'Well, if you can do it, I can do it.' It was very encouraging.

Mostly, I just chatted to them the way I talk to the kids on the buses, listening to what they have to say, and offering a bit about my own life and the difference that Jesus has made to me whenever it's appropriate. There were usually one or two prison officers around, and often they were listening in, too. I tried to feel at home in the prison environment, but I still got things wrong sometimes. One night I was told off by a prison officer for going into a cell and not 'double-locking' the door first, so that it couldn't be locked from the inside. He was angry because I could have been taken hostage – I'd put myself and others at risk – and I should have known better. I was still on a learning curve.

We ran a Youth Alpha course in the prison chapel, and that brought about some amazing conversations. One evening I was sitting next to a young man when we showed the DVD of *Nobody's Child*, and I could tell that something was stirring in him. When we stood up at the end he turned to me and said, 'Will you pray for me, John?' Then he put his hands on my shoulders and bent his head forward until our foreheads were touching. It looked a bit weird and people must have wondered what we were doing, but there was a sense of real contact. We prayed together and he asked Christ to come into his life and change it. It was such a privilege to share that moment with him.

Another evening a guy said to me, 'It's a great story, John, an amazing story, and you've done well for yourself. But I don't believe in what you believe in.'

I said to him, 'So what's your story, then, mate? 'Cos I can tell you're very angry and bitter about what's happened to you.'

'Yeah, I am,' he said. 'I came home from school one day and there was a note on the kitchen table from my mum and dad. They'd gone to Spain to live, and they said they wouldn't be coming back.'

He'd been left to fend for himself at the age of sixteen, and he was still filled with anger and resentment, and the feeling that he mattered so little to his own mum and dad that they just went off and left him. I said to him, 'Listen, whatever your parents think, God thinks you're amazing. He thinks you're a prince. And he never leaves, and he never walks out on you. People may let you down, but God never will.'

We saw some amazing changes in the young people we worked with in those institutions. I loved building them up and saying, 'God can use you like he's using me. You're so valuable and precious in his eyes.' I know the devil doesn't like that. He wants to see these young lives destroyed, and that's part of his plan. But God's plan is to save and rescue them and build them up, to his glory. He can give us back our past – 'I will repay you for the years the locusts have eaten' (Joel 2:25) – and he can give us a future too.

I had a great time as Prison Team Leader, and I loved to share my testimony, talk and take part in services, but after a while I realized that something was missing. I enjoyed working in the Young Offender

Institutions, but I was even more excited about working with the young people when they got out of prison, when they were back on the streets and facing all the temptations of their former lives. The institutions were closed communities, not the real outside world, and that was where I wanted to be and to work with them. I hesitated for a long time, but eventually I decided to talk to Andy Hawthorne about how I was feeling. To my surprise he told me that Steve (my replacement as leader of the Bus Ministry) and his wife wanted to move back to the south of England, and that they had been praying about their next move. Steve had got another job almost immediately and everything had fallen into place for them. Andy was pleased for them – but it meant that the buses were standing idle.

As soon as I heard that, I knew that I wanted my old job back. I had longed to support the prison ministry, but this wasn't my work. God had taught me another lesson: you can weigh everything up in terms of experience and suitability, and you can go off and do what you think you should be doing, but it may not be God's plan. Just as before, I had to accept that, even though I seemed to be admirably qualified for and suited to the work in human terms, it wasn't what God wanted me to do.

Maybe God will want me to work in prisons one day in the future. Maybe the timing wasn't right. Or maybe I just needed to learn that lesson – that nothing is wasted, and that there is no experience, however bad, that God can't take and use and turn into something beautiful for him. I still go into prisons to speak at special events, and of course I visit if young people ask me to, but it's not my main vision. Right now, the Bus Ministry is what I do, and I love being out on the street, working with young people and meeting them in their own area and their everyday lives. If I have any gifts in youth work – my ability to reach young people and understand their lives and talk to them honestly about the love of God – they come out of the damage of my past. My past is part of who I am.

Chapter 7

THE VICAR'S WIFE

By this time Gillian's work in our church was building up, and her faithful adherence to her vision was bearing fruit. She was always seeking to work on the renewal of faith within the church, combined with providing opportunities for those outside it to find faith. We both see so many damaged people outside the church, and we know that God can help them. That's why reaching people with the good news of Jesus has always been our passion.

We ran Alpha courses where people came to find God, and they built up the faith of the church family too. Recently we had a confirmation service for twelve adults, and the Bishop asked Gillian to provide a short history for each person. As she wrote those stories down, she was struck by what an amazing couple of pages they made. Several people had suffered abuse as children that had affected them as adults, and they had found freedom in Jesus for the first time in their lives. One woman said, 'Well, if I'd known that the Holy Spirit could heal me, I wouldn't have bothered with all those years of counselling!'

As we talked about it, we realized that it's easy – especially when your work is so closely linked with your faith – to get caught up in the routine and mundane parts of church life. It's good sometimes to reflect on what God is doing in people's lives. It's only when we look back on the road we have all travelled together as a church, that we see how far God has brought us. Nowadays we have a congregation of around seventy or eighty at the main service, plus about fifty children, and all age groups are represented.

It's great for me, because although the church is Gillian's field of mission and work, it's also my resting place, the place where I go to be fed, to share in fellowship with the church family, and to build up my own Christian life so that I have something to offer when I go out to do my work on the buses.

Part of Gillian's job includes being a governor of the church primary school in the parish, and as the vicar she also takes assemblies every week. It's a fantastic mission field. The children's response to her assemblies was so good that some of them said they'd like to come to Sunday School – but their parents didn't want to go to church and wouldn't bring them. So Gillian decided to take the Sunday School to the children, and started running a school club at lunchtime once a week. It's called FPW, or Funky Prayer Warriors (the children chose the name!), and around forty children attend. In fact, it's so popular that she's now struggling with the numbers – there isn't room to accommodate the next class coming up from the infants to the juniors, so she now needs to start another lunchtime session for these extra twenty children. There is one little boy with a sad little face who regularly pleads to be allowed to come to the club, but there simply hasn't been space.

Ours is an ordinary area, and some of these are tough kids, but they are lively and interested and they just absorb God. It's great that kids who aren't taken to church by their parents have responded so well to the opportunity to meet God and get to know his love. In one assembly Gillian asked, 'How do you know God is real?' A tough little lad of about ten put his hand up and answered, 'Because I can hear him in my heart.' I thought it was amazing that he was willing to say that in front of all his friends.

Another day Gillian showed the DVD of *Nobody's Child* to a class of eleven-year-olds, who were preparing to go up to secondary school. At the end, she noticed that one lad had tears in his eyes. He'd obviously identified with some of what he'd seen. In front of the whole class he put his hand up and said, 'I was going to run away before I saw that today, but I'm not going to do it now.'

It's an example of the way that sometimes our ministries overlap, and I get involved in what Gillian is doing. She was concerned for the young people in our own area, but the Bus Ministry can't get everywhere, so we sat down to think what we could provide for them. In the end we came up with an idea we'd tried successfully before, in Southampton – a non-alcoholic bar. That first bar is still doing well, with around 100 young people visiting it regularly, so we knew it could be done.

We identified a suitable space – a room just off the main church which was being used as a combined vestry and storage area. It doesn't bother me when I see parts of church buildings being used as cafés or shops – to me, a building is just a building. It's the people of God, filled with the Holy Spirit, who make it a church. This room was pretty untidy, full of old boxes and things, and it needed clearing out and redecorating, but we realized that between us we'd got the skills to do it fairly cheaply. Gillian and the girls cleared out the massive spiders; Sarah Green, one of our church family, worked out a wacky colour scheme and a group of them helped me do the painting and decorating; Andy Clements, who also works with me on the Bus Ministry, did the electrics, and Paul Cooper (our churchwarden) built the rest from scratch! I designed the bar and we installed a kitchen area and seating. We managed to get about £2,000 in grants from the Youth Parish Mission Fund, and that paid for some of the setting-up. We made it look just like an ordinary bar – we even have a big screen on one wall – and the only difference is that we serve 'Amethyst' non-alcoholic cocktails. The syrups are supplied by a specialist Christian company.

We're open every Saturday from 7.30 to 9.00 p.m., and we have at least two adults on duty. Alice was involved from the start, before God called her to Canada, and since then we have been joined by John and Sarah who have been a real blessing to the bar and, most importantly, to the young people. We make sure that the church is warm and lit, and we have another adult from the congregation on duty in there, because the young people have to walk through the church to reach the bar. When they open the door and see the bar for the first time, they're amazed! Usually we get around thirty people per night, but one evening recently we had over fifty, and they spilled out into the church and sat down there to chat. The people in the church kept telling them to go through into the bar, but they couldn't because there wasn't enough room!

Most of the young people who come have no Christian faith and they don't come to church. They just enjoy coming to the bar, chilling out with their friends. We don't have any specific activities, except for the occasional Quiz Night, just like you'd get in a pub. However, every week just before we close up, I run the equivalent of the God Slot – the kids call it John's Corner or John's Talk Time. I share my testimony or a story from the Bible, and we take prayer requests. There's no pressure on anyone to stay, but we never have anyone leaving early or missing it.

Another innovation in our church is something called Taste and See. It's a monthly event for local people, where we taste food from all over the world (or even a ham sandwich!) and have a speaker. They may share their testimony or talk about their work – for instance, we've had a couple talking about their work with abandoned children in China. We have the food part of the meeting in a lounge room, but we move through into the church to hear the speaker, because we aren't ashamed of being Christians and we want people to get used to being in church in a relaxed and unthreatening atmosphere.

I was the speaker on one occasion, and I was more nervous that night than I've ever been. It's one thing to share your testimony with a hall full of strangers, but it's something else to stand up and talk about yourself in front of the neighbours! I was quite happy when I looked out and saw that not many people were there, but when the church started filling up I got quite anxious. That week a woman came to church for the first time and told Gillian that she was there 'because of your husband's talk'. She had suffered a lot of rejection, and wanted to know how she could be free of it, because she knew it was damaging her life. Gillian explained to her that God can set us free, and she became a Christian that night.

We had one teenager who came to the bar regularly, and she brought her mum and dad along to a Taste and See session. It was wonderful to see the whole family there together, and to see her so excited about bringing them. She has trained as the bar manager, and she's growing in confidence all the time. She's soon going to be confirmed, and now her dad has started coming to church with her.

I enjoy my Saturday evenings, though it's bit of a busman's holiday for me – literally! I have a nice night off from working with young people on the Bus Ministry, and I spend it working with young people in the bar. Apart from the bar, I try not to get involved too much with the rest of the youth work in the church, because then I'd never get a break. For a long time I was involved with our Sunday morning young people's group, but I knew that I had to take time to be fed by God instead of giving out all the time. Still, I feel I should do something for the young people in my own church, as well as for those in the Greater Manchester area which is The Message's mission field. I have a commitment and a responsibility to help our own church family.

During the week I do my job – the administrative work for the bus, training new volunteers in everything from child protection legislation to anger management and youth work skills, visiting schools or prisons, and going out on the bus on some evenings. Meanwhile, Gillian is kept busy doing hers – church meetings, pastoral visiting, mentoring, counselling, preparing sermons and planning worship, and helping in the church school. Sometimes it can be a fight to fit everything in, especially when you live in a vicarage, which always seems to be open house. Gillian officially works part-time, but her hours can be very long, because you can't turn people away if they come to you in a crisis. There are so many needy, hurting people whose lives are in a mess; often they have never known any hope, and they need love and they need God. We have encouraged our church to become a place where everyone can find hope in Jesus.

One of the practical problems is that diocesan structures don't really cater for growing churches: staff are allocated according to the size of the parish, not according to how many people are actually coming to the church, or what kind of work is going on there. Other churches may be full of people who like to come to a service on a Sunday and maybe attend a mid-week group, but that's all. By contrast, our church is full of new Christians who have been so overcome by the power of God that they want to give their all. They want to live their lives for God, and that's absolutely wonderful – but it can mean a lot of work to channel their energy and enthusiasm. Add to that the number of personal problems that arise in any area where there's a certain amount of poverty and a fair few social issues, and there's always a lot going on. That not only adds to Gillian's workload, it also affects me and the girls. We have to work hard to find time to be a family.

There can sometimes be tensions if I have to work a weekend, or certain nights in the week, when Gillian has something in her diary, too. Most of her parish meetings are held in the evenings, and if it's a night when I'm working, they have to happen in the vicarage so she can be at home with Natalie and Leah. We have to think of them, too: we don't want our children to grow up thinking that mum and dad were so busy doing God's work that they had no time for them. The girls understand that we work hard because we want to help people and tell them about God, but we don't want them to grow up resenting it, so we have had to learn to schedule time as a family. The best times are when we go off for a bike ride together, or just have fun chatting about what they've been up to at school or playing with their friends. We have given our lives to serve God, but our children need our attention, too.

When Leah was seven or eight she started having problems at school. At first her teachers thought she might have a hearing problem, because her spelling was so unusual: even now she will write 'Richard' as 'frigud' for example. Tests confirmed that her hearing was OK, but that was just the start of a long and painful series of tests and assessments. Eventually she was diagnosed not just with dyslexia – problems with reading, writing and sequencing – but also with dyspraxia. This condition, which causes coordination difficulties (Leah has muscle weakness and a slight tremor in her left hand), has been called the 'hidden handicap'. It can cause severe social and educational problems for the child. Any parent who has had a child with special needs will know how difficult this can be within the school environment. Eventually we moved the girls to our church school, where the special educational needs support has been much better.

The diagnosis gives Leah a special link with me, because my own dyslexia wasn't identified until I was an adult. She knows that I understand her problems, and she can also see that I have come through and manage to run my life, even though reading and writing aren't my favourite activities. It hurts me when I see the social rejection which she suffers: other children sometimes leave her out of games because of her clumsiness, and she finds certain social situations difficult. I want so much to protect her, because I know what it feels like to stand on the edge of things, looking on. However, she has a firm faith, which is a tremendous joy for us. She makes up her own worship songs and they are always songs of praise: she is a little girl who has learned to trust God through her difficulties.

At night we always have a story, a chat and a prayer time with the girls separately, and Leah often needs extra time to talk about her day, because that's when she processes her difficulties and works out ways of dealing with things. But we have two children, and it has been hard for Natalie because Leah has needed so much attention. We realized this when Natalie said one night, 'If I tell you some stories about school, will you stay longer with me, too?' They teach us, and we learn.

Natalie is very quick-witted, and shares my wacky sense of humour. One day recently Leah and Gillian went out to do some shopping, but Natalie didn't want to go. 'Dad and me are going to do the housework, and he's promised we can put loud music on and be silly!' She was really excited at the prospect!

I find all this fascinating, because I never knew my parents, so I didn't know what to expect from my relationship with my own children. The girls say that I'm a softy, and they know they can wrap me round their little fingers. Gillian tends to be the disciplinarian in our house, because the girls know I can't bear to be hard on them. She imposes the same loving discipline that she had as a child, such as 'No pudding if you don't finish your dinner.' Natalie knows she only has to pull a silly sad face, and I'll melt and give in.

Working with young people as I do, I see children younger than my own who already have major problems. It makes me all the more determined to nurture my own family, and to enjoy the girls while they're young. I'm so proud of them, and I want to enjoy being their dad.

On Saturdays, if I'm not working, we make time as a family for shopping, outings or even (excitingly) housework! In the evening Gillian may share her sermon with me, so on Sunday I get a rerun – but I still have to try to look interested and enthusiastic about it. (I don't always manage it, and sometimes she catches me yawning.) I like to just sit there in the pew and take it all in, and pretend to myself that I haven't heard it all before, because it's my chance to learn and grow. I enjoy going to church and not being in charge, just being me – worshipping, taking in God's word and meeting up with the church family.

People laugh when I say that on Sundays I have to be the vicar's wife, but that's essentially what it is. It's my job to support Gillian, and I can do that in lots of ways. After the service she'll be chatting to people at the door, and I do my bit, sometimes talking to the young people, sometimes to the men, because some of them may find it difficult to relate to a female vicar. People often compare Gillian to Dawn French as the Vicar of Dibley because they both laugh a lot!

Quite often the girls will come up with some plan they've hatched with the other children, and say, 'Louise's mum says we can go and play at her house', because they've worked out that if Mum and Dad are both busy, we're more likely to agree. Later we realize we've been manoeuvred into plans we didn't quite understand at the time or weren't concentrating on!

Then we go home and have lunch, and after lunch it's time for family games – we all love board-games like Boggle, Monopoly, Battleships or The Game of Life. I love this relaxed family time, when we're all laughing and teasing each other and playing together. Gillian and I have always bounced ideas and jokes off each other, and the girls are picking up on that and joining in. Our house is a lovely, lively house, full of fun and laughter.

It's not all plain sailing. Ours is just a normal marriage – you don't get any short cuts just because she's a vicar – and we still have a few barneys. If we've had an argument on a Saturday night (yes, I know you're not supposed to let the sun go down on your anger, but we're only human and these things happen), it's all the harder to sit in church the next morning and listen to my wife preaching. I sit there in the pew with a face like I'm chewing a wasp, thinking, 'I'm not listening! I don't want to know!' I know it's childish, but it's hard to see her standing up there in a position of authority when we haven't resolved our differences. But somewhere about halfway through, it always comes home to me that Gillian is preaching the word of God, and that's what I'm listening to. (And she's not scoring any points off me.)

Occasionally being the 'vicar's wife' makes me want to do something outrageous – dance or light up a cigar or walk through the church with my pants on my head – anything wacky to ditch the image and prove that I'm just an ordinary person. (On second thoughts, maybe that last one wouldn't be very ordinary.) The problem is that there's a lot of pressure on clergy couples. There's an expectation that we'll always be there for people, offering counsel and support, and on one level that's exactly what we do, and it's a privilege to do it. But on another level we sometimes feel that when we have our own problems – like with Leah – it's difficult for us to find the support we need.

There are no days off when you live in a vicarage, and sometimes it feels as though we're living in a goldfish bowl – we're always under scrutiny. The doorbell is always ringing. Sometimes, on a hot summer day, I answer the door in a T-shirt, with all the tattoos and scars on show. If it's someone who doesn't know us, they generally say, 'Are *you* the vicar?' in disbelief, as if anyone looking like me couldn't possibly be.

'No, my wife is,' I reply.

'Your *wife* is?' they say, though whether they can't believe the vicar is a woman or they can't believe she's married to me, we never know.

Sometimes I'm tempted to sing, 'Yes, can I help you?' as if I'm singing the responses in a church, or to offer them a cucumber sandwich with the crusts cut off, just to debunk the whole 'life in the vicarage' image. Other times we say, 'Let's take the girls *out* for tea,' just to get away from the doorbell and the phone. It's not that we don't love our life, but occasionally we have to make space for us.

In fact, life's tricky enough just learning how to be a family. Gillian comes from a loving family, but I don't have any happy childhood memories to draw on. I only have bad memories of my foster homes, and though I was happy at Barnardo's, it wasn't a family environment, it was an institution, and the people who looked after us were professional staff. As a result, I always feel as if I might be getting things wrong. When Leah was born, I sent Gillian a Mother's Day card from me, because she was now a mother, and I didn't know that it was meant to come from the children. Christmas and birthdays are quite emotional times for me, because I didn't have many that were good when I was growing up. It was a part of the life that other people had, but was closed off to me. For a long time I didn't understand how it all worked: what did you have to do to make a fuss of someone on their birthday? What makes a family Christmas?

I still have little habits that hang on from the old days. It's a joke between me and Gillian that whenever I have new clothes, I keep wearing them: I take them off, put them through the wash and put them straight back on again. Gillian has nearly had to force me to change outfits, because as she says, other people won't know I've washed the clothes and put them back on! It's because I was never used to having a choice about what to put on: what I had was what I stood up in. I'm still a bit like a squirrel, collecting things and putting them away in a box or a bag. I've done a few counselling courses, and nowadays I understand that this sort of behaviour is typical of children who have been deprived – either materially (in terms of having no personal possessions) or emotionally (in terms of being starved of love). They hide things away because they are precious, and they think they will be taken away if they aren't guarded or hidden.

I also have a problem with packing for holidays or trips – I find it impossible to decide what to take with me. I've done ten charity bike rides in different places around the world, and when I arrive people always say, 'Where's the support team?' I reply, 'There's no team, just me.' And they say, 'So why have you got five suitcases?' It's because I've got five jumpers and twenty pairs of underpants and socks, even if I'm only away for a week. And in any case, when you're biking, you don't need an extensive and varied wardrobe – just your shorts and shirt, and you wash them and put them back on the next day. When we go away for the weekend as a family, Gillian laughs at me for insisting on taking every pair of shoes I own – even sandals, 'just in case', in the middle of winter! It's just that having enough clothes represents security for me.

I get a lot of support and understanding from Gillian and her family, and they've helped me to learn what family life is like. They've accepted me and made me feel a part of the family, and I'll always be grateful for that. Gillian's mum never takes sides – if Gillian rings her for a grumble or if we've had a row, she'll always ring and speak to me, too, so I won't feel as if I'm being excluded. Gillian's dad has been good, too, showing me how to do DIY jobs around the house, as a dad would do for a son of his own. Gillian's two sisters have become like sisters to me, and their families are part of my family, too.

Gillian and I try to work as a team, sharing the family responsibilities because we both have to juggle home and work in the same way. Even though Gillian is the vicar, leadership in the church is partly a joint effort. Sometimes I wish she could see me at work out on the bus in the evening, the way I'm able to see her when she's leading worship. It's not just that I'd like her to be proud of me, but I'd like her to see me doing what God has called me to do. She would love to come out on the bus with me, but we don't have babysitters for the children, so she prays for me at home. I'm proud of her, because I see that she's doing a good job, but I also see the Holy Spirit at work in her and through her. When she preaches she challenges and moves people, and the worship is amazing when you can feel that spiritual uplift when everyone is praising God wholeheartedly. We can share in that because we're there together.

Gillian rarely sees me at work, but sometimes I get that same feeling of being led by the Holy Spirit – that prompting of when to speak and when to be silent and listen; which kid needs attention; knowing the way to disarm the cocky and aggressive lads without putting them down or belittling them or robbing them of their fragile self-esteem. And we have our special moments, too, when someone who has never been interested in the God Slot comes upstairs and asks for prayer. I sometimes wish Gillian could be there to share those special moments. I often ring and ask her to pray during the evening, especially if something is kicking off. It's good to know that she's praying for my safety on the bus, and when I get home we really value being able to share together about our day. Church leadership can also be lonely, and we find it helpful to be able to offload to each other and pray together before we fall into bed at about midnight.

In 2006 we had a special treat, though – we were both invited to speak at Lee Abbey. It was great because that was where we met, so we had lots of happy memories of the place. It was a good moment to give thanks that God has blessed us with each other, and to realize how much we really do appreciate each other. We enjoyed working as a team. It was a long time since we'd been able to minister together outside of our home church, and it was good for me not to be the vicar's wife for once!

Chapter 8 　　　　 # LONG GRASS BOY

After I left Lee Abbey I was often invited to be a guest speaker. It was a bit of a shock: I'd never seen myself as one of the people who stood up and spoke at meetings. In fact, there was an absolute explosion of invitations for me to speak. People who had met me at Lee Abbey (I'd been there for two years, and a lot of guests had passed through in that time) had gone back to their own churches and told others about me, and the invitations started to flood in. I was nervous at first but I began to get used to it. It was as if God was mapping out a ministry for me, and I was pretty surprised. I'd never thought of myself as having a ministry – just a story.

I was mostly asked to speak at youth groups and Young Offender Institutions, and I think I've visited most of the prisons (adult and youth) in England. Young people always seemed eager to hear my testimony of how I became a Christian, coming from my background and experience. I always had to be careful not to let any mythology build up about me personally. I didn't want people saying, 'Oh, your story is amazing.' Everybody's story is amazing, whether you were good or bad beforehand, whether you were an axe-murderer or someone who fiddled their expenses;

whether you became a Christian suddenly or gradually. That's your testimony and it's the story of how Jesus came in and changed your life.

Then *Nobody's Child* was published, and it's since been translated into several other languages: Korean, Hungarian, German, Dutch and Thai. Suddenly my name was known all over the world. I was never comfortable with being put on any kind of pedestal. Sometimes I was introduced as 'John Robinson, the author of *Nobody's Child*'. Before the book came out, it was 'John Robinson, ex-gang member', or even, 'John Robinson, bus driver', but actually I was still just John – a man with a story to share about what God has done in my life.

Getting asked to be a speaker means that I've visited places and met people I would never have dreamed of encountering. Who would have thought that I would have fantastic opportunities to travel to such places as Malaysia, America, Singapore and Australia to share what God has done? I've been into schools and colleges, and one college even invited me to be their honorary chaplain – me, who left school at sixteen with no qualifications! I've spoken to Women's Fellowships where eighty-year-old ladies have faithfully prayed for the Streetwise project in Southampton, and for The Message, and for me and Gillian and the girls as a family. I've even spoken alongside Luis Palau at Festival Manchester. I was really nervous about that. Andy Hawthorne was speaking about the work of The Message Trust, and as part of his talk he asked me to share my testimony. I stood beside him on the stage and looked out at the crowd and thought, 'Can I really stand up and speak in front of all those people?' Then I realized that God had provided the opportunity, and so he would give me the confidence to do it. He uses ordinary men and women to do his work and spread his message of love. It was ordinary men and women who told me – and now I'm telling other people.

At first I was terrified that I'd get my words mixed up or repeat myself or forget what I was saying, but I found that once I got started, I got so fired up with what I wanted to share – that God's love is waiting and reaching out to all his children – that I forgot my nerves and the words just came flowing out. Nowadays I give talks at least once or twice a week, telling people about what God is doing. I love meeting interesting people from all walks of life. You couldn't have a better job, really!

The most extraordinary place I have ever spoken at, though, was in Australia. My friend Paul Webster and I have been best mates ever since we met at Lee Abbey. We've laughed and cried and prayed together, and even after we moved on – I went to Southampton and Paul went off and became a police officer – we kept in touch. Then Paul married his lovely wife Nicky and they felt that God was calling them to go to Australia to work with the Aboriginal people there, so they emigrated. We were determined not to lose touch, so I was delighted when Paul contacted me with a bright idea. Why didn't I come to Australia to do a charity bike-ride out there with him?

I've done about ten charity bike-rides now, and I love them. The first one I did was from Jerusalem to

Eilat in aid of the National Children's Homes (now called NCH Action for Children). I saw it advertised in a leaflet and I thought, 'I'd really like to do that.' You had to raise your own sponsorship (with a minimum of £2,000), and then you could join in an organized event with lots of other riders. I had to train hard in order to be fit enough to ride up to seventy miles a day, and by the time I got home I'd caught the charity bike-ride bug. It was a great way to travel, keep fit and also support a good cause.

I did two rides with Paul, the second one being in aid of The Message, which always needs donations to keep up the work it does, and it wouldn't be like the huge externally organized trips I'd been on before. This time it would just be me and Paul riding together. He also wanted me to speak at his church in Darwin and to a couple of school groups, and I could do a book-signing at a big Christian bookstore in Sydney. It sounded like a brilliant plan: we could do the bike ride together, and afterwards I could visit the Aboriginal people Paul works with. I assumed that it would be just like the work I was doing in the UK. Of course, it didn't work out quite like that.

I knew that the bike-ride was going to be pretty gruelling, and that I'd be suffering from jet lag when I arrived, so I planned to make the most of the flight – time to relax, read a book, watch a film, get some sleep – bliss. We stopped off in Singapore and I queued for an hour to make sure that I got a seat near the emergency exit, where there's always more leg-room, as I'm quite tall. On the plane I settled down, noticing that there was an empty seat next to me and a girl sitting on the outside. I stretched out and closed my eyes.

'No, you don't, John,' said God. 'That girl in the end seat needs to hear your story.'

'But, Lord!' (I was talking to him silently in my head now.) 'Couldn't I just have a nice glass of wine and a meal first?' The answer was the same.

I sneaked a sideways look at the girl and saw something in her face – maybe she'd just had a glass of wine to calm her nerves before the flight, or maybe it was something more than that. I said, 'Hi, my name's John,' and we shook hands. I realized at once that she was desperate for some conversation, and before long I knew a lot about her. She'd had a difficult life and had experienced all sorts of abuse and neglect, but she was going back to New Zealand to visit her family. I wondered what sort of welcome she was expecting.

Then she asked me about the book I was reading, *The Heavenly Man*. I told her it was a Christian book, and she said that some of her family used to go to church, but that over the years they had all given up on 'religion'.

'OK, Lord, that's my opening,' I thought. I told her about myself, and how Jesus had changed my life. When I'd finished there were tears trickling down her face.

'Thank you for telling me that,' she said. 'I wish I could believe the way you do.'

I didn't force the issue: it's God's job to touch people's hearts, not mine, but I was so glad that I'd made the effort to talk to her. If I hadn't bothered, she wouldn't have had that opportunity to think about what Jesus was offering. Perhaps I was just a link in the chain of contacts that would bring her to meet God – who knows? When I got off the plane in Sydney, I left my book behind, in the hope that she would pick it up and read it.

Sydney was amazingly hot. I looked like the typical Englishman, getting off the plane in a woolly jumper and carrying a coat! I got a taxi to the Koorong Christian Bookstore, where I was going to be staying in a flat over the shop. When I say it was a Christian bookstore, you shouldn't be thinking of a little high-street shop: it was more like an Asda superstore. People walked round it with shopping trolleys, it was so big. I gave a talk at the bookshop and did some book-signing (till the jet-lag caught up with me), and over the next couple of days I gave talks in some schools, too. It was all pretty much as I had expected, and I congratulated myself on settling in so well.

Travelling up to the Northern Territory was where the surprises began. I couldn't believe how far it was: a four-and-a-half-hour flight. I thought I was probably nearly home again! When I looked out of the window all I could see was sand, going on for ever.

We landed in Darwin after dark, and as I stood at the top of the plane steps waiting to get off, I saw a big ball of tumbleweed blow past. It was a bit different to Heathrow! Paul picked me up at the airport and we set off towards his home. After about half an hour he pulled off the main road onto a dirt track and stopped. He said, 'Let's get out of the car for a minute, John.'

I climbed out and stood there in the Australian

night. The heat was unbelievable, and the air was filled with the deafening chittering of insects. I saw a snake slither across the road in the headlights of the car, and then Paul switched them off. There was total blackness: not a street light or a house in sight, and no moon. I blinked for a moment and looked up, and then I saw the stars: more stars than I've ever seen in my life, millions of them, and the air was so clear that once my eyes had adjusted, I could see Paul by their light. He had come round to stand beside me and look up in wonder at the sky. I turned to him and gave him a hug.

'Paul, it's so good to see you, mate. Thanks so much for having me.'

I felt so grateful to God for bringing me here and giving me the chance to have all these experiences.

We drove to the house where Paul and his wife Nicky lived, at a school in an Aboriginal community where they were responsible for twelve Aboriginal boys. It looked like a building site on another rough dirt road and the annex they lived in was like a little cement shed with a tin roof and a tiny cubby-hole bathroom. They had used a curtain to partition off a part of the living space for me to sleep in, with a net curtain over the bed to keep off the mosquitoes and creepy-crawlies. We did a very gruelling ride on this trip in the Litchfield and Kakadu National Parks and the following year I returned to do the second ride.

By now Paul and Nicky had moved to live and work at a big school on the outskirts of Darwin. The school focuses on helping Aboriginal children receive an education and Paul's role was as a houseparent for these students who were boarders. It is a Christian secondary school where over 25 percent of the students are Aboriginal, coming from around 40 different communities and numerous language groups. For most of them, English is their second language – so you can imagine the educational challenges. Many of the children have special issues they have to deal with, coming as they do from a section of the Australian population which is often seriously disadvantaged with high drug and alcohol use and sickness, as well as high suicide rates and a lower life expectancy. Needless to say, Paul's job is demanding and I thought the school was doing a brilliant job, especially when I read the head teacher's account of their aims:

> Before any child can be responsive to learning, basic needs need to be met. Feeling loved, safe and healthy is a basis for self-respect, growth and being open to opportunities. If you have spent your life being abused, not eating healthy food, into drug abuse from an early age, solved problems through violence, have inappropriate models, have been raised with mixed and ambiguous values and no boundaries…how can you focus on learning to read and write in English?

That made perfect sense to me, and it spoke to all my experience in my own life and what I saw of the young people I was working with in Manchester. Reaching out to these youngsters and showing them the love of Jesus was the way to offer them the freedom and self-respect they needed. I could see that Paul and I were doing very similar work, even though we were on different sides of the world, and I really wanted to support him and Nicky all I could.

Two days after arriving we set off on the second bike-ride togethr – in the vast Kakadu National Park. We were aiming to do 240 kilometres (around 154 miles) on a route within the park. We'd both been sponsored by family, friends and local people, and we were determined not to let our supporters down, even though, as with the first ride the previous year, it would be tremendously hard work. We cycled together with Nicky driving the support car, and we all had walkie-talkies so we could keep in touch. On the radio we all had code names: I was called 'Mustn't Grumble', Paul was 'Sore Buttocks' and Nicky, who was pregnant, was 'Little Bump'. Once or twice we saw a light aircraft flying low overhead, and I can't imagine what the pilot thought as he overheard our radio conversations: 'Come in, Little Bump, this is Sore Buttocks. Is it time for a water stop yet?'

It was incredibly hot and humid, and although I had done lots of training and was pretty fit, I'd never anticipated anything like the demands that ride made on me. It was about 110 degrees Fahrenheit and 75 percent humidity by midday, and during the day we each drank around twelve litres of water just to keep hydrated. In fact, on one day I didn't drink enough, and I got really ill from dehydration. We covered the distance over three days, and I got sores in places I didn't know you could get sores! The sweat ran down me and stung my raw skin. Each night we returned to the cottage where we were staying, which was owned by two friends of Paul and Nicky. Then in the morning we put the bikes in the back of the support van and drove to our new starting-point.

Kakadu National Park is where some of the Australian parts of *Crocodile Dundee* were filmed. It's the most amazing place, with huge areas of floodplain grassland, billabongs alive with wading birds and masses of crocodiles. It's not just a wildlife haven, though – it's a UNESCO World Heritage Centre, with lots of important rock art sites and is said to have been continuously inhabited by Aboriginal people for 40,000 years.

As we rode, Paul filled me in on some of the background about the society where God had called him to work. When Europeans first discovered Australia at the end of the eighteenth century, their initial contact with the native people was not altogether peaceful. They brought with them European diseases (to which the indigenous people had no immunity) as well as alcohol and tobacco, which all had a destructive effect on the Aboriginal communities. The Europeans also started taking over the people's traditional homelands, and there were massacres of those who resisted this process. By the end of the nineteenth century, some have estimated that in parts of Australia as many as 80 per cent of the native people had died with the situation even worse in places like Tasmania.

Losing their traditional lands meant that the people couldn't reach their usual sources of food and water, and they became dependent on the white population for their livelihood. Very few Aboriginals were permitted citizenship of the new Australia (they didn't get the right to vote until the 1960s and their land rights were not acknowledged until the 1970s), and so they became a displaced people in their own country.

Nowadays around 70 per cent of the Aboriginal population live in the cities. The other 30 per cent who live in settlements in the outback – often on the sites of early Christian missions – suffer extreme poverty, unemployment, poor health and poor education, as well as rising rates of alcoholism and violence. Paul and Nicky and a couple of friends have started a church in an Aboriginal community, Knuckey Lagoon, which meets every Sunday evening, where they worship in an iron-roofed hall with open metal-mesh walls. They have good relationships with the people in the community and try to show the love of God in all they do, but there is so much need.

However, when I visited they were involved with running the church at another community – Bagot. At the end of the bike-ride Paul took me there to meet the people for myself. The government has given the people houses, but many would prefer to live in their traditional way and take their mattresses out onto the verandas so that they can sleep under the stars – and having seen those night skies, I can understand why. They light bonfires to cook over instead of using a stove, which some white neighbours think is a sign of uncivilized behaviour.

Changing people's traditional lifestyle like that is incredibly disruptive. The men who used to be the tribal leaders, whose hunting skills and wisdom would once have been vital to the community, now have nothing to do, and the boredom means many will sit around drinking grog and smoking. Walking

around the camp, I saw women gambling and drinking, and youngsters with a can of beer in one hand
and a can of solvent to sniff in the other.
Unemployment is very high, and people seem to have
no purpose in life, so they take refuge in whatever dis-
traction they can find.

Just like in England, where you get alcohol you get
violence, and it isn't limited to the Aboriginal people.
One night, in Bagot community, we were waiting to
lead a meeting on a disused basketball court in the
camp. It was close to the road and lit by a spotlight. An
Aboriginal man, who was very drunk, was playing the
guitar and I was about to preach, when another
Aboriginal man arrived on a motorbike. He got off
and bumped into a white man at the back of the
crowd. The man turned round and head-butted him
so hard that he fell to the floor unconscious. People
screamed, and we ran over to help him. When the
police arrived one of them looked at me, Paul and
Nicky and said, 'Why are you working with these people? They're always trouble.'

I wanted to shout at him, 'These people aren't
nothing, they're not wild dogs! Every one of them is
somebody's child, with hopes and fears and a life to
live. Every one is an individual, special to God.' The
police were really quite threatening, standing there
with their batons drawn – they seemed ready to react
with violence to the slightest wrong move. They were
so pristine in their smart uniforms, too, and such a
contrast to the scruffy and ragged Aboriginals in the
crowd. I felt that they saw me, a white man, as one of
them – but I wanted to be alongside the Aboriginals. I

knew what it was to be despised and outcast, and I identified with them much more than with the authority of the police.

I saw other instances of prejudice, too. Back in Darwin one day I went to get a drink from a public water fountain. A white guy was standing beside it and he said, 'Mate, you don't want to drink from that. An Aboriginal guy's just been drinking from it.'

I shrugged and had a drink anyway, and Paul said, 'Well, they've only got the same diseases we have.'

It's not surprising that these people felt that they didn't belong anywhere – turned out of their traditional lands, and treated with prejudice and suspicion in the cities. They were living on the fringes of society, often they were high on drink and drugs, they couldn't get jobs and most of them seemed to have lost all self-respect. I looked at them, and although I had grown up on the other side of the world, I recognized the pattern from my own life. I thought, 'I've been here before.' I felt rejected once, I was on the street with nowhere to go, dirty and scruffy and unwashed and smelly, ill and lonely, with no hope.

Yet look at me now. I'm surrounded by so much love – the love of God and the love of my family and friends. I wanted to sit down beside them and share some of that love with them, to tell them that there is hope, no matter how low you think you have sunk, because God never gives up on anyone.

The Aboriginals aren't the only people in need. One day Paul, Nicky and I were out and about in the Bagot community talking to some Aboriginal people when two white lads came up to us.

'All right, mate?' said one of them. 'Got any drugs on you?'

Generally I forget about the way I look, but I realized that they were judging by appearances. A white guy hanging out in the Aboriginal camp, covered in tattoos – I was obviously a drug dealer.

'No drugs,' I said. 'I've got something better.'

'Cool! What is it?'

'It's Jesus. And I can tell you that the buzz you get from God is so much better than anything you'll get from drugs.'

They shook their heads and went off – they clearly thought I was mad or off my head on drugs. I stopped and said a word of prayer for them – what pain were they trying to blot out, with their search for drugs? What had gone so wrong in their lives, that they wanted to get high? They were somebody's children, too.

I warmed to Paul and Nicky's work and I saw how much they were appreciated. It isn't just a case of giving money or material support – it's making relationships and treating people the way Jesus did, as whole, valuable individuals. I was reminded of John and Rose Lancaster and their belief in the mission which involves building relationships. One day we sat with a young girl who was dying of lung disease, and we held her hand and prayed for her. She gave me a turtle shell with a picture painted on it, as her way of saying thank you for being there and caring about her.

I had the privilege of preaching in the bare Aboriginal church in Bagot community. The floor was concrete, scattered with blood and glass where there had been a fight the night before, and smelling of dog mess and urine. There were bundles of old clothes in the corner, given by a charity and not collected. So much for my idea that I'd be talking to people in tidy church halls like the ones at home. I told them my story, and how I'd been in the dregs of society in England, without a job or a home or any family. I saw men and women weeping openly as they listened.

One man stood up and said, 'My story is like John's. I found Jesus and I found new hope. I've been off the grog for a while now, and my life is so much better. I know that God loves me, and that made all the difference.'

The people there gave me a nickname – Long Grass Boy. A 'long-grasser' is the equivalent of a person who is homeless and lives on the streets – or literally in the long grass in and around the city. For a people used to living and hunting in the bush in the remote communities, living in the 'long grass' is second nature, really. There are several communities in Darwin – places such as Knuckey Lagoon, Bagot, One Mile, Fifteen Mile and Minmarama – where Aboriginal people live in overcrowded houses, especially in the wet season when they come into town to be closer to amenities. However, in the dry season many of them move out again to live in the 'long grass' where they can hunt, fish, cook and drink without being bothered. The 'long-grassers' seem to be generally held in contempt even by Aboriginal people. Paul said I should be impressed: to be given an Aboriginal name is a great honour!

I was proud – it meant that I was accepted. Even

though my skin was a different colour, I had a strange accent and I came from the other side of the world, these people had recognized that I shared some of their experiences, and related to their problems. They were people who hurt the same, who cry the same, and who need to belong and be loved the same as me.

I had a great time in Australia, and it showed me even more clearly why I work with the Eden Bus Ministry, and why my heart is to go to people whom others regard as scum. I always want to have time for the people who are outcast, who are treated like a waste of space, because someone did that for me. I came back to England on fire for God and for my job, wanting to give more to my ministry, and to contact as many of the lost young people in our society as I can. Evangelism is a fancy word, but in fact it's just a willingness to relate to people and share what God has done for us.

Being an evangelist sounds like a highly skilled job, but fortunately God gives us all the training we need. As I found when I started giving talks, when the Holy Spirit is in our hearts, he gives us the confidence to talk about God's love, whether it's speaking to a hundred people or just one. The important thing is to be willing to listen to his prompting, and to make the effort even when we don't feel much like it.

I had another example of that not long ago. I'm a great fan of hot, spicy food, and for a special treat after an evening on the bus I sometimes stop off and buy a kebab to eat at home. One Friday evening I parked the car – which has the logo of The Message painted all over it – outside the shop and hurried in and ordered my kebab.

'What's that on your car?' asked the shop-owner. 'What do you do for a living?'

'Lord,' I prayed silently, 'it's been a long week. I've only come in for a kebab. I really don't want to get into a long conversation here.'

'Oh, it's a charity,' I said out loud.

'What sort?'

'A Christian charity.'

'So what do you do?'

I could smell my kebab and my mouth was watering, and I was thinking, 'I haven't got time to stop and explain all this. I just want to take my food home and eat it!'

Then I felt God saying to me, 'Come on, John! You can have your kebab later. You can warm it up in the microwave when you get home.'

I had an idea. I ran out to the car and got a copy of *Nobody's Child* and handed it over the counter.

'What's this?'

'It's about how I became a Christian.'

'I'm a Muslim.'

'That doesn't matter. Read the book if you want to. It's for you.'

I got my kebab. The next time I went in, the shop-owner said, 'Mr John, your book was amazing! It is great what God did in your life.' I'd made a new friend. And though I don't go in there very often, I keep being offered free kebabs – or at least I was, until Gillian put us all on a healthier diet!

I didn't expect to have the chance to witness to a

Muslim friend, but then, God specializes in the unexpected. It doesn't matter whether our contact is Muslim, Jewish or atheist – God shows us what he wants us to say. We may think we have nothing in common with someone – like the girl on the plane, the Aboriginal tribesman or the Muslim fast-food cook – but God has other ideas. My vision is to tell people about Jesus, and when I do that I find that I can relate to them and befriend them. I want to point people to the Saviour who can reach and transform their hearts and lives – whoever and wherever they are.

Chapter 9   # TRANSFORMING POWER

One of the most rewarding things about the work we do is seeing lives changed, and God's transforming power at work. I shouldn't be surprised – he did it in my life – but every time it happens it's such a buzz. Everybody feels it.

However, we have to be real, and we have to be honest with people about what we're offering here. In a sense, we're offering everything: a way back to God, a relationship with Jesus, the power of the Holy Spirit, eternal life – the whole package. It's pretty impressive.

But on the other hand, we're offering nothing. Your life isn't going to change overnight. Your dad isn't going to stop drinking, your mum's debts aren't going away, and you're not going to be transported off your rough estate to a life of luxury somewhere else. You'll still have to take the rap if you've got a court case hanging over you.

But God does have a plan for your life, and he has much, much better things in store for you. He'll give you the strength and courage and support to change your life, but he won't immediately turn you into a different person. It can be a hard slog.

I'm not afraid to challenge people when I think they are ready to accept Jesus into their lives. I once had two lads who had been coming on the bus for ages. I'd watched them growing up through their teenage years, and pretty wild years they'd been. One day I thought, 'I've got to tell them. They've been hearing the message – and my testimony – for years, and I've been telling them that God loves them.' So at the end of the God Slot I turned to them and said, 'Guys, it's time. God wants you to give your life to him tonight. Will you pray the prayer with me?' To my surprise, they both said yes. The bus was full that night, and in front of thirty or so of their mates, they stood up and said, 'I'm sorry for all the wrong stuff I've done. I want you to come into my life, Jesus.'

On the other hand, that isn't the only way to come to God. Although becoming a Christian is ultimately about each one of us deciding to invite Jesus into our lives as our Saviour, it isn't necessarily a sudden event like what happened to Paul on the road to Damascus. God deals with people as individuals – he doesn't have a single method of saving people, a sort of 'one size fits all'.

Take Steve – he's got a job as a joiner, these days, but he still comes to the bus. For a long time he was really loud and lairy when he came on in the evening, and he was a lad with a lot of issues. He could be quick to fire up and start a fight. But over time we've seen him settle down. He's got more confident, and less likely to get angry. He asked me for a copy of *Nobody's Child* and kept coming back to talk to me about it. I'm not sure about his faith level – he's never made a public commitment – but now he wants to be a team member on the bus. That's a life transformed, and I don't need to see Steve sign on the dotted line or make a public affirmation of faith to see that God is working in his life. He's ministering to the other young people in a very real way.

We can't judge anybody's Christianity or spirituality. Someone who's just lost their dad may not believe in God much that day. But the long journey of their faith is still going on. We do see lives changed, but it doesn't happen overnight. There was Arron, whose brother had died. I've seen him coming on the bus dribbling because he was on drugs, or drunk and fighting and shouting abuse. He used to be high as a kite: I've seen him run at the bus and up the side, nearly to the top. I used to think that one day he'd bounce right off the roof. But whenever he stayed for the God Slot he was listening and learning. Gradually we noticed that he was coming off the drugs, and getting more control. He could sit quietly and talk for longer periods. He learned to stand back when a fight kicked off, and had the self-control not to wade in and get involved. He even learned to ignore it when people tried to rile him. It was five years before Arron was ready to pray the prayer and give his life to Christ.

Now he's linked in with an Eden Project church, and he's going on with God in the way he understands. He may not be like me or you – he may still be smoking and drinking – but it's up to God to work at his pace in Arron's life. One day he said to me, 'I got drunk last night and I had a spliff.'

'And?' I said.

'Well, it's wrong. I'm a rubbish Christian.'

'No, you're not. You're just learning, step by step, like the rest of us.'

In fact, of course, he's come a long way. That's a quiet night compared to what he used to have. The point is that lives often don't change instantly, and if we put pressure on people to change overnight, we're setting them up to fail. I hate the term 'backsliding'. Who knows what work God is doing in people's lives? Some churches might not be able to cope with young Christians who have the occasional lapse like this, but God is the God of creation, and I'm sure he's big enough to cope with the odd drink. Being a Christian isn't about instantly being made holy – it's a gradual process of getting nearer to what God wants us to be.

All the same, God does change lives, and his transforming power brings hope to the hopeless and love to the lonely. We all have ups and downs. I always tell people not to look at me – I'm only human, and I'm bound to let you down. Look past me to God, because he'll never let you down.

One of the most humbling things when *Nobody's Child* was published was the huge number of letters and emails that poured into my office, telling me how the book had touched people's hearts. Most of the people who wrote to me had had some experience in their lives that made them relate to my story, and their stories make amazing reading, telling over and over again about the power of God to heal and save. Obviously we can't print them all here, but I would like to thank everybody who has taken the trouble to respond to me. It's been a great blessing to me to know that the book encouraged you.

I've included some of these letters and emails below, omitting any details that might identify the people concerned. I've tried to contact them all to get permission to print their testimonies here, but some of them have moved on. You know who you are, guys, and I hope you'll forgive me for sharing your stories, but you've been an encouragement and an inspiration to me, and I know you will be to many other people.

[1.] I was brought up in a Christian home, but I got involved in some pretty choice things after the death of my best friend because I thought I could do better on my own. After the death of two close friends I was ready to end it all. As I was standing on the banks of the Tyne ready to jump in, I felt something pull me back from the edge. When I turned round, no one was there...At this point, I thought no one cared about me, never mind love me. My brother took me to hear Steve Chalke speak (under much protest) and during the time that he was speaking, he looked straight at me and said, 'Do you realize God loves you?' I tried to ignore it, but it kept bugging me...I took some convincing that God didn't care what I'd done in the past and he was willing to forget it all.

From this point I was going to live 110 per cent for God. It was the hardest thing ever. All the people back home knew what I had done and weren't as willing to forget as God was. I changed churches and now I am a youth leader, help out at the kids' club and have just taken five young people to Festival Manchester.

Lately though I felt really troubled by my past...then I read your book and realized that you could give loads out but not take enough in. I realized I was still in need of healing from the past, in terms of learning how to trust people again, after the rejection from the church. Looking back, though, I do believe that God had to take me down that road in order to become the person I am now and to find the faith that is so precious to me. Thank you for writing the book and for being a willing servant of God.

[2.] I recently read your book with great interest and was wondering if I might possibly meet you and find out more about the work you do with young people. I work as a nurse/drug worker for a Substance Misuse service where we do our best to help our using clients, but I know there is something (or rather, someone) more powerful out there than a methadone script! God bless you.

[3.] Greetings, John. I have just read your book in our school library. Wow, what an amazing story of God's redemption. Thank you for taking the time and having the courage to share your life. Your story encourages me when I see the lives of some young people heading in the wrong direction.

My life was a little difficult when my parents broke up when I was twelve years old. They were frightening times and [there was] some violence and I grew up in a church community where at that time hardly any other families had broken up. I suppose a breakdown at thirty-five was the accumulation of the pain, fear and isolation one can feel. Like you, God has brought healing in my life. I am happily married with two children...Yes, God has blessed and healed me and used me to encourage and support others going through the trauma [of] family break-ups. I do, however, still stand a little closer to the edge than others, but that just keeps me hanging on more tightly to Jesus! Praise God for his mercy and healing grace.

[4.] To begin with I'm not a book critic and born-again Christian, just someone who believes in God and Jesus (still learning) and is part of a little church...I read your book in two days between the fun-filled Noddy rides and family worships [at Spring Harvest] and I couldn't put it down.

Even though I never had a functional childhood myself (my father having a mental illness) – mind you, not many people do, these days – nothing can compare with the sadness of yours. And I did have tears in my eyes when reading about your childhood and what you went through. I did feel, John, that you were writing from the heart and some of your personality shone through. And you have a good sense of humour (I liked the bit about the cats). I did feel it was your own words...While reading your book I noticed there were a lot of references and stories relating to your tattoos – I feel body art tells a story all by itself, especially how people judge others by appearances, though honestly I know I have done it myself...

I hope you feel encouraged on how inspiring your book is and how I have been thinking about my own life.

Take care, from an inspired reader.

[5.] Anyway here I am, twenty years old, no family, a criminal record I'm not proud of and I'm so lost. Obviously I've just given you a small amount of my past but the fact is I've been lost all my life. It's so scary when you're on your own. I have no one, no friends, nothing. Because of the arson I can't get an address for my tag so I'll have to do another four and half months. I've been in the system so long now, I hate it but I don't know how to live outside of it. I've heard you have come into the prison before, it would be nice to talk to you, I know you're busy and have loads to do but you're a success story. It's nice to think I could be someone. Maybe you could help me.

[6.] I have just read *Nobody's Child* in one sitting. My husband and I became foster carers fourteen months ago. When I read your book I was so moved – that foster carers could behave so badly, but that God had always been with you, you just needed to ask him in. I have been aware that God was an OK guy since I was a little girl, but began to realize that I needed to commit to him as I grew...

Your story has moved me deeply...This morning in church our minister was using the theme of discipleship...he showed me his guide notes for the service, and there was a gap where he had pencilled in 'story' with a question-mark by it. He joked and said, 'I knew the Lord would fill the gap!' He then asked all the children to come to the front so that I could tell them your story. There was a moment when I thought I would break down because I started by saying that there was a little baby who couldn't live with his mum because she was unable to look after him, so he had to live with foster carers. At this point our Jade, who is just nine, put up her hand and said, 'Like me.' I thought of the contrast between your attic and her bright pink room with teddies and fairies everywhere, and I prayed for strength!

It worked – I kept the tale short and simple but was able to get across the point that God loved them all and he would help them – and in turn would shine through them to help others. Thank you so much for sharing your life. My prayers are with you and your family, and all the youth work you are currently involved with. We are currently caring for a fifteen-year-old, and the circles she moves in could certainly use a bus.

Yours in Christ...

[7.] I have just finished reading your book and I felt I should write to you.

I was moved by your book and it brought back many memories from my upbringing when I was younger. I also lived a rather unstable childhood and still sometimes feel the effects today.

One of the key points in your book which really hit a nerve was when you wrote, 'No one knows how great or how long-lasting the damage is when a child is fearful and insecure and unloved from his earliest days'. This really touched me as, although I now have a great group of friends and support...I sometimes find it really hard to appreciate them as I'm always fearful that it will not last. I sometimes find it hard to tell people as well, as I don't want them to feel that I'm in a 'bad place' and struggling, because that's not the case. I am healed, but sometimes it still hurts.

I became a Christian last year...and since then my life has changed so much! I am now helping to lead lots of youth groups for young Christians...helping them live for and worship God...This email is really just to thank you for writing a book which helped me to feel more 'human'.

[8.] Having just read *Nobody's Child* for the third time, I felt that I had to write to you to say how inspiring I found it. After having spent six months in prison at Springhill, I can echo the sentiment that having a belief in Christ does change lives.

It was during my time at Springhill that I re-found my faith in the Lord. When I was sentenced I felt that my whole world had come to an end and was totally depressed, feeling how much I had let my family and friends down. But within a couple of weeks I realized what had been missing from my life for the past twenty-five years...I am pleased to say that a copy of your book is doing the rounds at HM Prison Springhill...I am hoping that once my statutory six months are completed, to help in some way in the Lord's work there and in other prisons locally. The Lord is doing great work in the prisons in this country and I feel that in the coming years we will see many miracles done in his name. Yours in the Christ...

[9.] I have just finished reading your book *Nobody's Child* and I just want to tell you what a profound impact it has had on me, and I just had to let you know how happy I am that God has used your terrible and traumatic childhood, to end up working out to show his incredible glory in your life and the lives of those you meet...

I specialize in teaching dyslexic teenagers...I think that a lack of literacy has a lot to do with kids becoming disaffected and displaying anti-social behaviour.

I have been a Christian since I was about eight years old, and although I have always had a really deep faith in Jesus, I never really enjoyed being in church, worship music, sermons etc. That has all changed now!...I was baptized (at the same time as my mum) on Easter Sunday. I am now feeling so full of joy, it's just unbelievable. I feel like I want to do something practical and meaningful in my Christian life now.

As I read your book, I just related so much to where you were coming from. You are so down to earth and so sensible in what you say, and I love your sense of humour! Some parts of your book made me want to laugh out loud, and the next minute I was sitting there with tears streaming down my face. I have a very good friend who is (outwardly) successful and well off, but who had a really traumatic childhood and it really struck me through what you said that he is going to need a lot of time in which to heal the emotional scars of his childhood. Your book has really inspired me – praise God!

As for your tattoos, don't worry about people misjudging you – it says somewhere in the Bible that man looks at the outward appearance, but God looks on the heart [1 Samuel 16:7]. That is what is really important.

I hope you don't mind me emailing you, but I

thought you might appreciate some feedback about how your book has really touched me, at a special time in my life.

[10.] I am currently serving a sentence at *****, and I do a group called Befrienders. We go to the Chapel to sing hymns and pray. So this one particular night one of the chaplains showed us your video of how you became a Christian. I thought the video was deep and I thought you were very brave to actually do a video and explain in the way that you did. Since coming to prison I have found going to the Chapel very interesting and now I have started praying and I think I'm starting to find God...Hopefully when I leave this place I will take the Lord with me and I hope that my life will have changed and I'm able to say No to drugs and crime.

Me and a few other lads in here were wondering if it is possible for you to come and speak to us in person and help us believe like you have.

Sometimes I used to think I had it hard but when I saw your video it made me think about all the things I had and the things that you and other people didn't have, and I have started to appreciate that.

[11.] I hope you don't mind me writing to you. However, I have just finished reading your book, *Nobody's Child*, which I bought recently at Spring Harvest. I just wanted to say thank you to you for your honesty and courage in openly sharing so much so well of your life through this book. I am certain your book is a ministry in itself to whoever reads it and will prove to be a gateway for God to work in lives and hearts in a variety of ways. In particular, I feel it will prove a useful tool for those who have been affected by childhood abuse and are grappling in adulthood to come to terms with it.

In my professional life I am a Social Worker. I have worked in Child Protection in the past and now work as an adoption worker for a voluntary agency. As you may know, the vast majority of children placed for adoption come with a history of abuse and so this continues to be a major focus for my work. I am therefore very aware of the things which tragically happened to you.

It was wonderful to hear how God nevertheless had his hand on your life and kept you through it all to bring you to the point you are at now. One of the things I intend to do is to share your book with colleagues who do not have a faith...I am also trying to arrange for your book to be included in our church bookstall.

What I mainly wanted to say, though, was that I have been personally lifted and challenged through reading your book which is a huge encouragement and, though very painful to read in places, is a wonderful testimony to the work of God's grace and power.

[12.] Thank you so much for replying. Your story is similar to mine. I am a 'part' Aboriginal woman from Australia. I was literally taken out of my mother's arms and placed in a home, away from siblings, then on to foster care. (At the age of sixteen I discovered that one of my foster-brothers was my real brother.) I was placed in a non-indigenous Christian foster home and was subjected to horrific child abuse, in the name of

God. Apparently I was a child of the devil. The rituals to get the devil out of me were sick. The reason I was placed in care was because of my Aboriginality. There was a policy in Australia at the time to place 'half' kids in care, with the assumption to 'breed out' the Aboriginal in them and make them white. I, like you, couldn't tell the welfare and they didn't seem to notice anyway. I tried to tell people at church what was happening, but they told the foster parents after telling me I was an ungrateful sinner.

You can imagine the outcome. I was placed in a couple of Girls' Homes but I felt safer living in the park. I, like you, have a Master's in life from living on the street. Even though I felt lonely, I had a sense of freedom. At nineteen, I was violently raped and stabbed. I had a daughter and she was then taken from me by Christians. The guy who raped me was a Christian as well. I then 'progressed' to a violent marriage. That ended and I went head first into another one. Obviously this was becoming a bad habit...I am now married again to a wonderful man. We have a foster child, who we are adopting with his parents' consent...All of this is God's plan...

When I read my welfare file, I was devastated. I was thirty-seven years old. That's when I found out about my Aboriginal heritage. Not long after, I met my own daughter. You can imagine the emotional rollercoaster I was on. During this time, I had a dream. In the dream, Jesus came and took my hand. He led me back through my past and told me He would help me heal the pain. This has happened. I relived everything, but also transformed everything. Some things I had forgotten or suppressed. So I feel like I know your path. It sounds similar to mine...

I never got to meet my mother, however we did talk on the phone before she died. She and I had throat cancer at the same time. She died and I received a miracle. I had no surgery.

I have to say that even though I had a violent, cruel upbringing, I always knew God was with me...I have been fortunate to heal with my foster mother. She asked forgiveness and so did I. I don't have anything to do with her now, but I am at peace with the situation.

I believe that God has a purpose for me. He has transformed my life. Like you, I was told by experts that they couldn't understand why someone who has gone through so much is not an alcoholic, a drug addict or a suicide victim. I have attempted suicide three times. When I realized my attempts had failed, I was depressed – I couldn't even get that right. I have tried drink and drugs, but I like to be in control, like you.

So you see, your book is important for people like me. I have bought six copies because I have friends who have been through similar stuff and your book is so hopeful. *Thank you*...Your book is an inspiration to me and to others.

[13.] Hi from Cambodia where I am serving with WEC International among street children. Just to say how great reading your life story was. I read it all in one go. I believe there should be a copy of *Nobody's Child* in every prison cell in the UK.

God used one line from the book to speak to me. I

broke down and cried when I got to the bottom of the page where it says, 'You haven't failed here. You've sown the seed. Now it's up to me, not you.' For some time I have been wondering if my five years' work among the street kids of Phnom Penh had been a success. I was so encouraged through those words.

The Lord bless you, John, it's a great work he has called you to.

[14.] It is very sad that the local authority's care system failed you. They failed my family too. My mother was abusive to all her children as far back as I can remember. There was no love and much aggression and violence. My father was an alcoholic and spent long periods in prison. They were divorced by the time I was six years old...

Fear played a huge part in our lives. People visiting were unaware that there were children in the house as we were too frightened to make noise...It was not long after we moved to his house that my stepfather began to sexually abuse me. Also my brother was taken into care and did not return until he was seventeen. I later found out that we children were all on the 'at risk' register, but once my brother was gone we never saw another social worker...I ran away at seventeen years old to the police who said that the abuse from my stepfather was unprovable and therefore it was his word against mine...

I moved to this area and followed my dream to train as a nurse. I qualified and worked as a staff nurse despite suffering from anorexia and many psychosomatic illnesses...I have had numerous hospital admissions and very nearly died several times due to suicide attempts. I do believe that God has saved me many times...

I am glad that you are doing such powerful work amongst the youth in Manchester; I will pray for you and the 'ghosts' that still haunt you. I will also pray for the valuable work you are doing. Please pray for me as I try to work through the c**p in my head. I often believe that I must be evil to have had such an awful life and that the pain, bitterness and anger is my punishment. I so want to be well, to really love my husband, have a family of my own and to do what God wants me to do.

[15.] Hello, well I read your book *Nobody's Child* and funnily enough it's the first book I ever read and finished. I'm still wondering why but that wasn't the reason I wrote. I suppose it's because I know every inch of your life and I feel like I can relate to what you say but in a different way...I don't go to pubs and drink but I'm drinking under age, and no licence, and there's loads more, I can't say a lot because I'm in prison, well a young offenders, which ain't much different. And I'm out on the 18th and I feel like I'm going into a black tunnel, if you see what I mean, and it being my third time in here I don't really want to come back...Hope you get this and have the time to write back because I feel like I know you. I know that seems stupid but for someone who hates to read to pick this book out of millions, and it wasn't given to me, near to my release, it means something. Great people are hard to find...from another 'Nobody's Child'.

[16.] I am writing after having just read your book, *Nobody's Child*. We share some childhood stuff and I found the book took me in compassion into your own story as well as touching my own life in many places. I wanted to get in touch to join the queue (that great British tradition) of those who encourage you and wish you well for your ministry.

The book jumped out at me from a bookstall at a recent Black Stump festival (similar to Soul Survivor). The first thing I noticed was my photo on the front cover coupled with the error in the title. OK, it's not really me, but it looks like me as a gangly young teenager, complete with the 'I wish I wasn't here' sadness that I wore for most of my childhood. And the error in the title? For me it would have been called 'Everybody's Child'. The vulnerability that came from extreme violence from the woman in whose care I lived as a four- and five-year-old made me anyone's for the taking and I lived under further violence and sexual abuse from many people until I was fifteen years old and left that town.

Some time after I came to my present ministry I met a man who had been a senior manager for the organization that ran the Boys' Home I lived in when I was fifteen and sixteen. When we identified the link with each other he said, 'I remember you. You used to sit in your room not wanting to talk with anyone. Whenever I came to visit they had to go and get you and you would come out and say Hello and disappear into your room again.' I recently met the boy I grew up with over my back fence until we were teenagers. His words were, 'Whenever I came round to your place you were sitting in your room looking sad. We knew there was something wrong in your house but didn't know what it was.'

Perhaps from these stories you can see why the cover of your book hit me. The trauma of my life had lain hidden in my memory somewhere until I was in my early forties, just over ten years ago. Since then I've been on a pretty terrible journey of remembering and checking stuff out with my family and people who knew me back then. I work through the painful stuff by writing poetry which I read to my wife, fall in a heap, and God slowly gets me back to normal by healing the past. I came to Black Stump with the next poem coming to completion in my notebook, so with a head full of stuff I didn't want to remember I walked into the bookstall. And I met myself in the cover of your book. And I've met a bit more of myself in its pages...

I lived in the UK for a few years...and started doing part-time prison chaplaincy...In the prison I found men who had grown up like me – it brings tears to my eyes even as I write of it and remember them...

The comments made by the prison chaplain that you write about were very hurtful, even to me as I read them. [In *Nobody's Child* I wrote about a prison chaplain who visited Lee Abbey and said that in her view, everyone who was in prison deserved to be there.] I can only imagine the pain that those words brought to your heart. My time in the Boys' Home with a bunch of other kids in strife with the law came about under pretty weird circumstances...The unholy things that had been poured into my life for so many years, and by so many people, started to come out in anti-social and illegal behaviour even before I was a teenager. I don't think I have to convince you that many and probably most people in prison are really there on a foundation of other people's crime. And that proportion increases markedly with young offenders. That chaplain's words are so distant from the reality of so many people...

My son is now twenty-three and it is scary to see how many young people I work with in this gaol who are younger than he is. Their stories are too much like mine – or yours. And sometimes I see God work miracles of healing in them, just as I have known miracles of healing in my own life. And when the healing happens the crime just falls off them...

It is people like us, the broken and the almost destroyed whom God has rescued, who find ourselves running back to the world of pain from which we came, to do for others as some earlier servants of God did for us.

Reading these letters challenges me all over again. I pray that each of these people is still going on with God, and I pray that they know that he will never let them go, just as he has never let me go, even in the darkest times.

Chapter 10

GOD'S FAMILY

Over the past few years the Bus Ministry has expanded. We're busy every evening of the week, going into new areas like Old Trafford and Lower Broughton, and wherever we go, we ask for prayer support. This is because we are working in very volatile areas, where violence and aggression are the norm, and we never know what will happen. In fact there have been very few attacks on the buses – in six years they've been broken into maybe five or six times – but each attack has done thousands of pounds' worth of damage.

We're not told in the Bible that we might have trouble when we're working for the Lord – the Bible specifically says that we *will* have trouble. But over and over again we read that Jesus said, 'Don't be afraid.' We know that God is walking with us and protecting us. After seventeen years of doing outreach work, I know that it can sometimes be dangerous. But before I became a Christian, living the life I led then, I was in danger every day. So I don't worry about it. There have been plenty of times in the Bus Ministry when I've felt threatened and in danger, and I do have faith that God will protect me. But at the same time I believe that God has given me a brain and intends me to use it. So

I must keep looking around to see what's happening, and use all my training and experience and human skill to take sensible precautions to protect the bus, the team, myself and the young people we work with.

Of course, there are some things that are completely unpredictable. Once a brick was thrown from a bridge through the bus's windscreen while it was travelling along a road: that was incredibly dangerous, and it was only by God's grace that the young mum driving the bus – who happened to be pregnant at the time – wasn't hurt. I've been head-butted for no reason. Another time, I was putting stuff away and a young guy came up and pushed me up against the side of the bus and smacked me round the head for not allowing someone on the bus with drugs. We've had bricks thrown against the side of the bus as we're driving away at the end of an evening, and once I saw a brick bounce off straight back at the guy who threw it, which made him run off!

When there are a lot of young people around, sometimes there's a bit of play fighting, but that can easily develop into a real fight, if someone really gets hurt and tempers blaze up. We always try to ignore stuff that's being done just to get attention, but we have to take notice of anything that looks like developing into something serious. I think the fact that we've had so little trouble is due to a combination of prayer and good teamwork. How the team deal with situations is incredibly important – sometimes you can defuse a situation just with good humour and assertive body language. It's when you let your guard down that things get dangerous.

Maybe two girls are having a row, and really going at each other, and then their parents come out and join in the slanging match, and it turns into a major community fight, and the bus gets caught up in it. Our instinct is always to try to sort things out and be peacemakers, but sometimes that's just not appropriate. One night something was starting off and a young guy came over to me as I stood in the bus doorway. I knew him, and he was mixed up with a crowd who were heavily into drink and drugs. He said, 'John, we respect you for coming down here, but this is a situation you need to keep out of. Don't get involved.' I appreciated his advice. I could have dived in but I didn't want to get beaten up – or worse – for the sake of getting involved in something I didn't understand. My job was to protect the young people and the team on the bus, so we closed the doors and drove round the corner to safety.

Later on I was driving round the area with a friend, and I saw a boy I knew had been involved. He told me the situation had calmed down. One guy had been stabbed in the arm, but he didn't seem to think that was a big deal.

I said, 'Are you all right, mate?'

He answered, 'John, this is Manchester.'

In other words, what else do you expect? This is the way it is. He was completely resigned to the idea that you just had to accept it. I felt so sad for him. I thought, 'There's so much more. God has got so much more in store for you than living like this.'

We meet all kinds of young people when we're doing this work, and often we get to know them quite well. Even the kids with no major problems at home seem to find their teenage years tough, as they try to establish their independence and find out who they want to be. Others have horrific problems – parents in prison, parents who have died, parents who aren't interested in them because they have their own drug, alcohol or relationship problems. When you talk to those kids you can feel the fear, the rejection and the unresolved grief and anger that underlie their behaviour. They keep those emotions hidden, but sometimes, when you show them love, they react in quite a violent way, because they don't know how to respond or how to express their feelings.

As we meet them and listen to their stories, we realize that many of these young people have experienced all sorts of damage. It can have a significant effect when we start working with them and give them the opportunity to talk and open up in a safe environment. How can they offload some of this stuff without being violent, verbally or physically? There are negative emotions: anger, bitterness, pride, fear, domination, resentment, and hatred of women or men. We see mental illnesses: anxiety, depression, eating disorders, phobias, and addictions to alcohol and drugs. There's occult involvement: sometimes they are addicted to horror films or supernatural ideas. Sometimes they have been cursed – not necessarily by evil spirits but just by being told that they're scum, they're useless. There's physical and sexual abuse. Things can be done to young people that they can't deal with, so they block them out and try to forget.

Have you ever seen those government adverts for

literacy and numeracy, which say, 'Get rid of your gremlins'? I think they're brilliant. You see people in ordinary situations, with an ugly little green man who follows them around, taunting them and saying, 'You're really stupid because you can't do maths.' It's so true to life – we all have things we're sensitive about, and the things people have said to us play over and over in our heads like the voice of the gremlin.

It's as if everyone has a sort of emotional cellar where we all chuck all our pain and emotional damage and lock it away in the dark, because we don't want to deal with it. But we know it's there, and it affects the way we react to things in our everyday life. The young lad I mentioned in Chapter 5, who couldn't read, might have had no problem with me asking him to leave the bus for smoking – either he'd have put out his fag or he'd have got off the bus. But when I stupidly said, 'Can't you read that sign?' I touched a nerve, and he kicked off. It wasn't just that he was embarrassed that he couldn't read. I bet he'd been teased and belittled and told he was stupid, and he'd tried to lock away all the hurt he'd felt. Then I opened the door with that remark, and all the anger came pouring out.

Some kids are so volatile, they react to the slightest word or look. They're filled with anger in response to what has happened in their lives. They can't live in freedom until God has dealt with the damage. I think there's a lesson for all of us here. Even when we're Christians, we can't live a godly life if we're ignoring what's in that cellar. We have to allow God to heal us, and to clear it out bit by bit. Stuff still happens to us, and we still get hurt and rejected at times. If we lock the hurt away, we're storing up trouble for the future. If we bring it to God we can get rid of it, and receive his healing and restoration.

It makes me look at myself and ask, 'What do I need to get straightened out?' I make sure I bring things to God, because there I know that I'm accepted. I know that God sees me as a man of God, a prince, someone who wants to be righteous, to have integrity, to become Christlike. Of course, things are going to go wrong from time to time, but I want always to go on walking with him. I never want to give up. 'I have fought the good fight, I have finished the race, I have kept the faith' (2 Timothy 4:7). Even if I have to crawl on my hands and knees over the finish line, I want to finish the race. I look at the tasks and the ministry that God has given to me, and I try to assess them. How am I doing in my work, my faith, and my family life?

For us as a family all those things are linked. Gillian is a wife, a mother to the girls, and a pastor to her people. I am a husband, a father to the girls, and I have my work in the Bus Ministry, the non-alcoholic bar and speaking engagements. When I look at the lives of some of the young people I meet on the streets, and the life I want to give Leah and Natalie, I'm struck by the contrast. It makes me all the more concerned to nurture and care for my girls, and to surround them with love and security.

How do you learn to be a dad, when you've never had one? When you've never seen that relationship up close? I want to be the best dad that I can be, and my children are helping to teach me. They tell me if they're upset with me, if I haven't listened properly to them or not spent enough time with them. Whatever the girls do – whether or not they succeed in the world's terms, whether or not they go to university or get married or get good jobs – I'll be proud of them. I want to say to them, 'I'm always going to love you and support you, no matter what happens.' I'm learning more about God by being a father myself. I want my girls to be able to tell me anything: I won't be shocked. If they've done something wrong I might be disappointed, but it's never going to stop me loving them with all my heart. Feeling like that has helped me to understand God's unconditional love for all of us.

Leah and Natalie are so important to me. Gillian pointed out that although she has a special place in my heart as my wife, and we are 'one flesh' in God's eyes because we are married, nevertheless the children have given me something I've never known before: a blood relationship. I've never had anyone who could say, 'You've got your mum's eyes or your dad's laugh' – I don't know anything about my family. But with the girls we can see family likenesses coming out: Natalie has a sense of humour just like mine, and sometimes Leah pulls a face just like I do. It's a precious bond which has healed a sore place in my heart.

Because I had no family whatsoever, for years the closest people to me were my church family. There were older men and women in the church who took me on as you would a foster child and nurtured me in the faith. Even now that I'm married, I still depend on my Christian friends. We've known Richard and Beth

Bissett for a long time, and they've seen us through lots of ups and downs. I often call them, jokingly, Mum and Dad (even though they're younger than me), because they treat me as if I'm part of the family, and their daughter Chloe calls me her brother. Sue and Derek Crookes and their daughters Olivia and Esther have been friends to us, and I can always go round to them for love, support and friendship. I can't count the times I've dropped in and Sue has fed me with cheese on toast or beans, in between telling me off about the hours I'm working! They accept me as I am, and it's hard for people to realize how healing that is, when you've never had a family of your own. I'm always aware of that gap in my growing-up years, when all I knew about myself was that my parents didn't want me. To be accepted by my Christian family is so important as a support network, and it encourages and challenges me too. Every church family we have belonged to, including the present one, has helped me so much with the love and support they've given me.

My friends at work are a support, too – even the guys in the office who keep up a constant flow of practical jokes (they've got me on a number of occasions and I've had to think up a good one in return). Having that kind of light-hearted fun together, as well as sharing the sad times and praying together, tells me that I'm accepted, part of a network of loving, fun-loving, supportive friendships.

The other thing that's helpful is mentoring relationships. Mike Edson, the warden at Lee Abbey, was one of my earliest mentors; my friend Ash, a doctor who has now moved away from Manchester, was another. Ash and I used to meet up once a week to talk and pray together, and we became accountable to each other, even though he came from quite a different background to mine. He is a marvellous man of great faith and integrity. There are other people I'm accountable to, however formally or informally, through having a pint and a chat with Andy Hawthorne, or even meetings at work with my line manager. It helps that they're all Christians; I'm accountable to them for different parts of my life, but I'm accountable to God for all of it. Often the most useful thing the mentor can give you is a sense of proportion. I set high standards for myself and sometimes I feel guilty about things. They offer an objective view and a different perspective, and maybe it turns out to be not such a big deal after all. At other times they might rebuke me in a loving way. That's what being in God's family is like – you have people who don't judge you but get alongside you and point out where things might be going wrong.

I've realized that I'm growing in my family life as a husband and father, learning more and more about being gracious, patient, understanding and loving. And our life as a small family reflects the bigger story of our lives as brothers and sisters in Christ, in the Christian family with God as our Father. Just as we care for and nurture our children, so we need to nurture new Christians when they come into God's family. Sometimes at the end of an evening on the bus, I ring Andy Hawthorne and Gillian and say, 'Three young people gave their lives to Christ on the bus tonight.' It's great, but what happens afterwards? In the weeks that follow, are they getting nurtured? Are they getting released from the stuff that's gone on in their past? They need people alongside them – befrienders, mentors and teachers. That's the job of the church, to offer discipling and nurturing.

That's why our Eden Project churches are so important, because they know their local communities and they are ready to be accepting and supportive of these new Christians. Encouragement is so important. They need people who will say, 'It's OK if you get it wrong sometimes.' If you become a Christian on a tough estate where people have known you for years while you've been growing up, and they've seen all the crazy things you've done, they're not likely to take you too seriously. They're more likely to say, 'Yeah, whatever – that's not going to change you.' That's when the doubts creep in, and it's important to have people alongside you who know how hard it can be.

I'm so grateful that there were people who took me in as a new Christian and put up with me as I painfully learned how to behave, to love, to take responsibility, and all the rest of it. My own journey wasn't an easy one, and I don't pretend that becoming a Christian waved a magic wand and 'fixed' me and all my problems. There are times even now when I'm painfully aware of the gaps in my past; when Gillian rings her mum and I know that – kind though her mum and dad are to me – I don't have the same support. I don't want to keep repeating this, but it's hard to convey how deep that absence of family goes. Plenty of kids are brought up in care, but generally they know something about their families. They usually have some contact with some family members – grandparents or aunts or uncles. They know that they belong in a family, even if circumstances (illness or prison or other problems) have caused them to be removed. I was definitely unusual – even thirty years ago – in having no contact with any family at all.

I can't explain in words what it meant when I stood at the door of the children's home and the staff said, 'Go inside, John. Your mum's not coming.' For a long time I reacted by pushing people away: I was so afraid of being rejected, and a bit of me couldn't believe that anyone could love me. But patiently, day by day, God is fixing that. He's clearing out that corner of my emotional cellar, and helping me to move on. I know that God is healing me, yet the memory of the pain is still there, and there are no words for the sick feeling that no one wanted me.

I think that's what people relate to when I tell my story; anyone who has known rejection understands the feeling. A new member of our church used to be a teaching assistant at our church school. She never went into the school assembly herself, but she says she remembers the children coming out and saying how good Gillian's assemblies were. One day she asked a boy what that day's assembly had been about, and he said, 'The vicar told us about her husband. He had nobody to love him till God loved him and she loved him.' That simple account stuck in her mind, and a couple of years later she came to church because she remembered and it touched her so much.

When I talk to young people who have heard my testimony, it's always that loneliness and rejection that they mention. They may feel so broken and so lost that they believe that nobody cares – they're a statistic, a no-hoper with no prospects, worthless. When they see someone from similar circumstances whose life has changed, it gives them hope. 'If you can do it,' they think, 'maybe I can, too.'

But we need to show them the love of God in action. It's no good telling them how special they are, and that God loves them, if there's no action to prove it. If they're hungry, we need to give them some food – and not an out-of-date sandwich from Asda, but something special – a sandwich on a plate with a garnish, or the best biscuits in the cupboard. It has to be the best, because it's making the point that it's God's love we're passing on.

I believe that if Jesus were here today he'd be in the bars and on the streets with the homeless, the drinkers, the drug addicts and the prostitutes. People were always telling him that he shouldn't be mixing with those awful people. I was an awful person, too, but Jesus found me, and he did it through the people who reached out to me. They didn't preach at me, but they fed me, and one young man put his arm round me – how many people would do that to a dirty, smelly, homeless person? I want to do that for other people, showing them the love of God.

That doesn't mean that I want to set myself up as anything special. God uses ordinary people to do his work, and I'm just the same as everyone else. When you see moths flying round a lamp, they aren't attracted to the base or the shade or the bulb – they're attracted to the light that shines out from it. I want people to be attracted to the light of the Holy Spirit shining through me.

That's the simplicity of the gospel. Jesus said, if someone's hungry, feed them. If someone's hurting, comfort them. If they're naked, clothe them. I don't want to be super-spiritual, but sometimes we get bogged down in plans and systems and meetings. If we knew someone was hungry, we'd offer them a meal. If I know a young person is homeless, I'll try to arrange some accommodation. If someone's hurting I want to comfort them, because so many people have comforted me over the years. They've had to be strong to do that, because I didn't find it easy to make relationships. A rejected person will reject other people, and a hurt person will hurt other people. Sometimes it's the only way of behaving that they know, because it's all they've ever experienced. You need to be loved before you know how to love.

Understanding that is a help when you're dealing with young people on the buses night after night, and wondering, 'Why are they behaving like that when we're only here to help them?' It's learned behaviour. Someone who has never known love scarcely recognizes it when it's first offered. The foundation of our selves – our self-hood, our self-esteem – is to know that we're loved. If you don't know that, if you feel rejected and that nobody cares about you, you feel like a nobody. Sometimes I look at the young people I work with and I think that God has a plan for them; they just don't know it yet. They're filled with hurt and there's a lot of work to be done in their lives – becoming a Christian is only the beginning.

I believe God has a plan for my life, too. Any father wants the best for his child, and God wants that for me. I'm entering a new season in my life. God has worked on my stubbornness and pride and my desire to do things my own way. He's brought me such a long way and taken me to places I never thought I'd see – spiritually as well as geographically. He's shown me my good points as well as my bad ones, making me aware of when I've gone wrong but never condemning me. He's encouraged me and told me he's pleased with me. The one thing I have always felt is God saying, 'I will always love you.' One of my favourite hymns is an old one – 'Amazing Grace'. It says, '...that saved a wretch like me'. I'm not a wretch any more, because God has been chiselling off all my rough edges (and he's still doing it). He has healed me, and the more he heals, the more I'm able to do. Every day when we get out of bed, there's a new thing God wants to teach us, and we just have to look out for it.

I'll never give up on God, because he never gives up on me. Even in my darkest moments, when the rejections of the past have threatened to overwhelm me, I've always had a deep certainty that God has been there and will never leave me. He says, 'You're not Nobody's Child, you're Somebody's Child – you belong to me. Life may be tough, but I'll always walk beside you and guide you. You can trust me because I'm your Father.' My own Father, finally!

That's the kind of love I want to take to the lost young people I meet. I don't kid myself that I can give them the answers to all their problems. I see so many kids who are hurting and I know I can't do anything about it. I've had to learn to do my best, to offer them friendship, to tell them about the love of Jesus, and then to let go. Only God can break into that cycle of rejection and pain, in his timing, not mine. Their destiny isn't in my hands; I just need the patience to keep praying that they will hold on to God. I know that God won't let them down; he will reach them and see them through.

Lots of them have troubled family lives, absent or abusive parents, or like me, no parents at all. Maybe their parents are doing the best they can in the face of their own troubled lives. From a human perspective, everyone is someone's child, because someone gave birth to us. When things have gone wrong, it's a relief to know that we can be born again. Even if our parents are dead or estranged, even if we don't know who they are, we have a Father in heaven who loves us and cares for us. Everyone is Somebody's Child, and that Somebody is God.

THE MESSAGE

John's work with the **Eden Bus Ministry** is just part of The Message Trust who have been working hard in Manchester for the last 15 years and, in partnership are seeing crime come down and Churches grow right across the region.

As the vision grows and the fruit increases they need more people than ever to stand with them. If you can help in any way or would like to receive regular prayer updates, please contact:

The Message Trust,
PO Box 151,
Manchester,
M22 4YY

www.message.org.uk.

CONTACT ME

After an amazing seven years with the Message, Gillian and I have felt God's call to move on. We are currently training and seeking God for our next step.

If you would like to contact me to know more about becoming a Christian, or if you would like to see a testimony video, you can write to me at:

John Robinson
Eden Bus Manager
PO Box 151
Manchester
M22 4YY

jrsomebodyschild@hotmail.com